INDIAN NATIONALISM

INDIAN NATIONALISM

ITS ORIGIN, HISTORY, AND IDEALS

BY

K. M. PANIKKAR

GYAN

Published by

Gyan Publishing House
5, Ansari Road
Daryaganj, New Delhi-110002
Phone: 011-47034999, 9811692060
E-mail: books@gyanbooks.com

Distribution Network
gyanbooks.com
India, USA, Canada, UK, Australia

ISBN: 978-81-212-7357-2 (HB)
First Published, 1920

2nd Impression 2024

Printed at: Gyan Press, Delhi.

INDIAN NATIONALISM
Author: K. M. PANIKKAR

INDIAN NATIONALISM

ITS ORIGIN, HISTORY, AND IDEALS

BY

K. M. PANIKKAR, B.A.

OF MADRAS

SOMETIME DIXON SCHOLAR AT CHRIST CHURCH, OXFORD

AND

AN ENGLISHMAN

1920

THE FAITH PRESS

22 BUCKINGHAM STREET, CHARING CROSS, W.C.2

MR PANIKKAR

DEDICATES

HIS UNDIVIDED SHARE IN THIS WORK

TO

"OLD OXFORD DAYS, 1914–1918"

He gratefully acknowledges his indebtedness to a member of New College, Oxford, for many valuable suggestions.

Both authors owe much to Mr D. B. Jayatilaka, of Ceylon. His sympathy and help have been primary factors in the writing of this book.

The Editor has received, from an authoritative source, the subjoined note on the constitution of the political organisation known as the Indian National Congress :—

"The Indian National Congress is a wholly democratic body. Anybody, who is a British subject, subscribes to its constitution and aim (self-government within the Empire), is above twenty-one years of age and pays a delegation fee of Rs.10 is eligible as a delegate. The delegates are elected by the Provincial and District Committees, which are widely representative bodies, and other public bodies affiliated to the Congress, such as the Home Rule Leagues, and also in open public meetings called for the purpose. There is no obstacle to the entry of anyone who complies with the conditions mentioned above."

When the Russian Revolution—fatally misunderstood—confronted us with novel formulæ, we proffered unto it grave assurances that its novelties were mere variants of English orthodoxy. In our zeal to seem friendly, we even professed to jettison Imperialism. Happily, we parted with nothing valuable, for the Imperialism we then verbally abhorred was not the one Imperialism worth having and keeping,—the Imperialism which completes that forgotten Freedom which is our lost strength.

Freedom,—*that* is the vital word. Governments exist to make and keep men free. That is their vocation. If they turn away from it, they become unmoralised powers, and divest themselves of authority, for only by Freedom can political power be moralised, only *through* Freedom can the divine authority of Government come to it. This Empire of ours must become the political form of a general conscience: it cannot become this unless it becomes a unity which everywhere intends Freedom.

England's history is an autobiography of Freedom. There should be no need in England to-day for an Englishman to write a defence of Freedom. Yet there is much need. This, however, is not the place for that defence. I may not now do more than make public profession of the political faith that impassions me.

In politics and industry, Freedom—the self-

government of the individual in and through society—is the first, the final, the consummating value.

For *that* Freedom no "good government" can be a substitute. The offer of that or any similar substitute, if not merely opportunist, implies ignorance or denial of man's spiritual nature. Freedom is so nearly *everything*, that without it other things are scarcely worth talking about. When a new demand for Freedom reaches us, our prudence always moves us to ask, "Are these people fit for Freedom?" The frailty of human nature in me makes that prudence a provocation. "Fit for Freedom"—who *is* fit for Freedom? Are we English people fit for Freedom? If there be anyone who thinks we are, let him adduce, from our present position and from the history of the last four years, evidence of our fitness. And, however fit we be, have we the political capacity to judge of another people's fitness? We assume, of course, that Freedom should everywhere assume some English form, and when we ask, "Are these people fit for Freedom?" the democracy that we know in England is the practical norm that we have in mind. To that norm we would have the Soviet Republic adjust herself, towards that norm we are timorously trying to guide India's millions. In each case we would establish Freedom in an exotic form. I hope I am a good patriot, but I am bound to confess I cannot bring myself to

PREFATORY NOTES

ON IMPERIALISM AND NATIONALISM

IT is my good fortune to have a friend. Profoundly learned in the earliest mythologies, he lives (for the more part) in that remote and unfrequented darkness which we conveniently designate "pre-history." The other day he came near to the haunts of modern men, and said to me something like this:

"At first the Empire was a mere supremacy. This form of Imperialism became obsolete,—supremacy was given, not a moral *content,* but a moral *objective.* Of this half-moralised conception, Lord Milner is the principal representative. It marked a step in the right direction, but it is not sufficient unto the needs of to-day, for it can hardly consist with the newly-emergent claims of Nationality. We must make it quite clear, in words and deeds, that the norm, the *telos,* of the Empire is something more than a benevolent supremacy,—is a vital synthesis of free peoples, an integration of Nationalities in and through Freedom. If we do not do this at once, we shall prepare for ourselves much trouble."

I listened and I agreed. Years ago the new Imperialism which my friend désiderates had been the burden of an evening's talk with John MacNeill, and I had heard him say, " We will listen to *you* : we will not listen to any English politician." I had resumed the story in many a letter to another Irishman,—in letters which became unavailingly known in Downing Street. Whispers from a new life in West Africa had reached me. I had listened to Eastern men while they exhibited to me the difference between the England that spoke through Whitehall and the England they had been taught to trust. I had been told of a continent in mourning when Tilak was imprisoned and ablaze with bonfires when he was released. I knew of disappointment in Burma, of resentment in Ceylon, of smothered dislike in Egypt. What could I do but agree with my friend ? He had told the truth. Turning an occasional eye from (let us say) Attys to Tilak, he had discerned the Empire's vital need.

Now the opportunity has come to me to write a few words prefatory to this book on Indian Nationalism. My task is an easy one. I have to do little more than emphasise the large conception towards which the authors have worked. That conception makes the book much more than a plea for Indian Nationalism. It is virtually a plea for a new Imperialism, and it marks a new stage in the development of our doctrine of the Empire.

believe that the world exists in order that it may be Anglicised. In no land can Freedom live except with a native life, and from that life she should assume her local form.

"Are these people fit for Freedom?"

If we ponder justly the constant vigilance, the unwearying energy, the unselfishness, the large brotherliness which are involved in fitness for Freedom, that question is one to which we shall address ourselves with much humble-mindedness. The truth of the matter is this:

> No fitness for Freedom is more than initiatory, and—on the whole—a demand for Freedom is a proof of fitness.

There is little more to be said.

Nationality is very like personality. What the latter is in an individual, that—or something similar—is the former in a people. Men often speak as though Nationalism were pathological—a disease in the body politic. It is not a disease, it is a sign of health. The world being what it is, the growth of a subject-people into national self-consciousness is a *normal* growth,—not merely something that often happens, but something that *ought* to happen.

What, then, of the Empire and its unity? *This.*

The Empire is not—as it is made to seem in Ceylon—a besmirched ark which may not be touched, and the essential unity of it can be a local energy otherwise than in an imported administration. The Empire is a polity which intends Freedom and the distinctive unity of it in a common loyalty to Freedom.

The Empire is a polity which intends Freedom. When we say this we are not giving to a political institution an adventitious value borrowed from private thoughts and hopes. Rather are we summarising a history and expressing a meaning.

Nationalism within the Empire, then, is not a negation of "the imperial idea," but a fulfilment of it. In it, local forms of life are becoming (as it were) consubstantial with that life which has created the Empire's distinctive character. Why, then, seek to depress it?

One hears again the answering words "unity" and "danger." On the whole, Nationalism will be a danger only if we insist that the unity of the Empire shall remain half-moralised. In the relations which subsist between the Motherland and the Dominions, the unity of the Empire has a form which approximates to the normal form, and that approximate form has lately proved its excellence. Why should we hesitate to make the unity of the Empire similarly approximate elsewhere?

No doubt there are differences. "Anzacs," for instance, are bone of our bone, flesh of our flesh. Hindus are of another breed. Yes, there are differences, but are they relevant? Freedom is a catholic value, and can unify, in a common loyalty to herself, peoples who are not akin.

My friend was right. There is a great work of imperial reconstruction waiting for us. We have to adjust the structure of the Empire to new developments of life. Through a new Freedom we have to establish a new unity. This *can* be done, and it *should* be done.

Now for a practical rule:

> Reconstruction should approximate to these two norms—the Dominion, and the national unit as a political whole.

(1) When one looks at the map of Asia it is hardly possible to doubt that, one day, the several territories of the Empire in Southern Asia will be self-governing parts of one great Eastern Dominion.

Why not move at once towards that inevitable term? For instance, if the Burmese people desire to be brought within the scope of the new provisions for the government of India, why not bring them within?

(2) In any given case, the "national unit" is the area defined by the national form of self-consciousness. In the case of Ireland, for instance, the unit is Ireland,—Ireland as a whole.

It may be that, in some part of the area thus defined, the national form of self-consciousness is not predominant. That may be a reason for temporary constitutional provisions of an exceptional kind: it is not, *per se,* a ground for dealing with the national unit otherwise than as a whole.

If a grant of self-government be limited to those parts of a national unit wherein the national form of self-consciousness is predominant, there is, in that grant, no recognition of "the national idea," but rather disregard (if not negation) thereof.

Recognition of "the national unit as a political whole" is one thing. The distribution of political power within that whole is quite another thing.

29th *November* 1919

CONTENTS

INTRODUCTION

Primarily, this book is neither a defence nor a criticism of a policy,—it is an account of a people's awakening.

There seems to be in human nature some original perversity which preordains, for every national movement that is a *growth*, three stages of maltreatment. At first it is treated with indifference, then it is ridiculed, then it is abused. Not until it has outlived these experiences of adolescence will men deal with it on its merits.

The national movement in the life of India is no longer adolescent. It cannot be ignored and it has survived ridicule. As for abuse, which has been plentiful,—that is an unwitting and involuntary homage to the strength of it, and is evidence of blindness in its opponents rather than proof of weakness in itself. To-day, Indian Nationalism is one of the great political movements of the world. Those who speak for it have established their right to be heard. No one says that the movement is immaculate, no one says that all its advocates have always been wise. But the leaders of the Indian peoples can and do claim that the movement they represent

A

is a *real* movement, not a factitious one. The strength of it is not in the fantasies of dreamers, not in the conspiracies of aberrant agitators, but in a spiritual awakening,—in an upward outreaching of a people's life. Because the movement is thus real, it has a right to be judged on its merits, and it will not defer to any other kind of judgment.

The movement is real. A vehement and well-known opponent of it[1] has admitted that each of the three Viceroys who have governed India during the last thirteen years has refused to confront it with mere negation. Two of these men were Unionist politicians; the other was a Civil Servant who had been trained in diplomacy. In no one of them could men suppose any predisposition towards Nationalism, yet each was constrained to incur the reproach of Nationalism. Why? These were not the men to go out of their way towards novel experiments in Freedom, yet each of them did take a step towards an experiment of that kind. Once more—Why? Members of the most masterful race on earth, beset by a potent and splendid tradition of mastery, they would not have yielded to mere force, or have betrayed their trust to an insurrection,—the small steps which brought upon them much reproach were not motived by fear. They *moved* because they discerned in Nationalism something greater

[1] Sir John Rees.

than the pressure they felt. They recognised in it a valid political thought.

Bear this in mind,—to-day, even those in India who contend most strongly against Nationalism are conditional Home Rulers. They no longer pretend that the peoples of India can or should be held in leading-strings for ever. The doctrine of "perpetual tutelage" lives only a secret life in the prejudices of men. It is no longer propounded publicly or defended publicly,—at least, not in India.

Not with bated breath, then, do the peoples of India now speak to their compatriots in the Empire. They are no longer petitioners to a Government,—they are applicants to their peers. Within them also the thoughts which have made the greatness of England, and have defined for the Empire a splendid possibility, have become a quickening energy and an uplifting hope. What shall be the Eastern form of England's great tradition? A bureaucracy ruling restive millions? That could not be permanent: while it lasted it would impoverish England's own thoughts. Rather would one hope to see the freedom which has made England's manhood so strong become an equal strength in the East.

Do not let it be thought that when Indians speak of Freedom they are babbling of some foreign thing which can never become native.

Indian Nationalism is not mere aping of a Western fashion. On the western edge of the hemisphere English life has become the garden of Freedom, and England her fortress, but the healthful seeds which have there brought forth so rich a harvest were not a gift to England alone. They are potencies in every human heart; wherever they grow, their life is *native.* And they are growing to-day in India,—growing fast. Let it not be said that in the eastern half of the Empire there is no room for them to grow!

CHAPTER I

THE POLITICAL UNITY OF INDIA

THE Indian National Movement claims to be the voice of India's progressing life. Like every other national movement, it presupposes a certain unity, —an integrating life, a common hope, a common Motherland. Those who oppose the movement say, "Show us that unity!" Then, without waiting for a reply, they go on to tell us that the required unity does not exist—they point to racial and religious diversity, to the Wars which incessantly devastated until a foreign strength, furthered by Justice, made the *Pax Britannica* an unearned boon. India, they say, has never had political unity, —it has not yet become the common Motherland of the Indian peoples, those peoples have not yet the unity of common life. The very word "India," we are told, is a foreign word—the adjective of it designates the descendants of Algonquins and Aztecs as well as the subjects of the *Kaiser-i-Hind*, —and grave pens pretend inadequate demonstrations that India has no other unity than the unity given to it from above by the British Government.[1]

[1] Their scheme of life for the Indian peoples includes loyalty, but not patriotism—at least, not *Indian* patriotism.

"Show us the Unity!" Those who speak for the Indian National Movement accept the challenge. This chapter is an answer to it.

In his learned and interesting book on the fundamental unity of India, Professor Radhakumud Mookerji has admirably shown that the conception of India as a political unity is no novel phantasy, born of modern "unrest." We cannot do better than avail ourselves of his work.

"Even such an old book as the *Rig-Veda*, one of the oldest literary records of humanity, reveals conscious and fervent attempts made by the Ṛiṣis, those profoundly wise organisers of Hindu polity and culture, to visualise the unity of their mother country, nay, to transfigure the mother earth into a living deity and enshrine her in the loving heart of the worshippers. This is best illustrated by the famous river-hymn of the *Rig-Veda*, where the various rivers of the Punjab, the perennial streams of plenty and good to which the country owes so much, which were at once the highways of commerce and culture alike, are deified by a grateful imagination and receive the nation's worship and homage. As the mind of the devotee contemplates in love and reverence those formative, beneficent agencies of nature contributing from time eternal to the making of his country, it naturally traverses the entire area of his native land and grasps an image of the whole as a visible unit and form. Certainly a better and simpler, a more convenient and significant formula could not be invented for the perception of the fatherland as one indivisible unit than the following prayer:

"O ye Ganga, Yamuna, Sarasvati, Śutudri, and Paruṣṇi, receive ye my prayers!"[1]

It calls up at once in the mind's eye a picture of the whole Vedic India, and fulfils in a remarkable way the poet's purpose behind it of awakening the people's consciousness to the fundamental unity of their country. Nay, it does more: it elevates and refines patriotism itself into religion. To think of the mother country, to adore her as the visible giver of all good, becomes a religious duty; the fatherland is allotted its rightful place in the nation's daily prayers. The river-hymn of the *Rig-Veda* therefore presents the first national conception of Indian unity, such as it was. It was necessarily conditioned by the geographical horizon which in that age seems to have been confined by the snowy mountains in the north, the Indus and the range of Suleiman mountains in the west, the Indus or the seas in the south, and the valley of the Jumna and the Ganges in the east.[2]

As the influence of the Aryans extended farther

[1] Ganga = Ganges. Yamuna = Jumna. Śutudri = Sutlej. Paruṣṇi = Ravi.

[2] *The Fundamental Unity of India (from Hindu sources)*, Radhakumud Mookerji, M.A., pp. 20-23.

and farther over India, the sacred unity of the homeland also extended, until at last it included the whole of India.

It is noteworthy that the chief places of pilgrimage in India are Hardwar, Benares, Puri, Ramesvaram and Dwarka. Hardwar lies at the very foot of the Himalayas, Benares is at the heart of Hindustan, Puri is on the coast of Orissa, Ramesvaram is in the extreme south, and Dwarka is on the west coast.

India was thus mapped out by holy places, and, although these lay far apart from each other, the practice of making pilgrimages from one to another give them a religious unity. The land was covered by a sacred network, and this made the land itself *one*—in all its distances, in all its diversity, one and indivisible.

Sanskrit literature abounds with evidence that, centuries and centuries ago, the diversified lands of India were apprehended as a *whole*, as a sacred unity. And that *whole* was not only a religious whole: as apprehended by love, it was also political.

Not long ago a member of Parliament—well known for his sympathy with India—told an Oxford audience that (until lately) he had been under the impression that Indian History began in the tenth century. Unfortunately, such ignorance is not exceptional in England. This explains the prevalence and persistence of that greatest of all historical misconceptions,—the misconception that India had no unitary existence until Clive and his successors gradually gave it a kind of unity under British rule.

"Indian History began in the tenth century"! The Indian Motherland counts her years by millenniums, and though much of her life be irrevokable, that which has become perpetual in history is the perduring inspiration of her sons.

The history of India is not, as it is often thought to be, a mere story of the rise and fall of kings, a *Police Gazette* of political crime, a mere chronicle of war and intrigue. In glory or disaster, it is always the *one* land that triumphs or endures, and even years of anarchy receive the greatness of tragedy from a unity which then suffers contradiction.

From the beginning until now, Unity—the "Intelligible Word" in human affairs—has been moving upon the face of the Indian abyss, gradually winning it from chaos into a reasonable and general order. The British unification is but one phase of a work which began long before Britain was heard of.

We will not go back more than twenty-two centuries. In the year 325 B.C. the larger part of India depended upon one imperial crown. Megasthenes, the Greek, who resided for some time at the court of Chandragupta, has left us an account in which we can discern an administration that would have done credit to the eighteenth century's best enlightenment. Asoka, the grandson of that emperor, was overlord of all India, and edicts still extant show the wide extent of his dominions. Eight hundred years later, a famous Chinese Pilgrim—Fa Hian—found the whole of India under the sway of the second monarch of the Gupta dynasty. To our no small gain, Fa-Hian was an exact observer and faithful recorder, and in his careful pages we can still see the Hindustan of the Gupta kings. The wealth and prosperity which that wandering Buddhist saw around him roused his enthusiasm—the liberty of the people moved him to admiration. Few, indeed, are the comparisons in which fifth-century India would be a bad second.

After the empire which Fa-Hian saw came the empire of Vikramaditya and Harsha. To that age all Indians look back with equal pride. They look back to it somewhat as Englishmen do to "the spacious days of great Elizabeth," for it was the age of Kalidasa, the greatest of Indian poets,—of Varahamihira, the greatest Hindu astronomer,—of Dhanvantari, the deified master of medicine and surgery.

The day came when a foreign race brought to India, on victorious arms, another religion and another sovereignty. The Tartar invasions gave to India Mohammadan rulers. Did the unity of India vanish ? No : even when the land was torn by a hundred wars, unity perdured in a deep sentiment which unnumbered centuries had made stronger than the storms of a day. That sentiment even took possession of India's new masters. It moved the great Akbar to seek for a new religious synthesis: it sent Aurangazeb forth on his southern expeditions.

An alien faith was dominant: the *imperium* was in alien hands. But days were coming in which the undying unity of India was to manifest itself, not only as a social fact, but also (in heroic patriotism) as a *Native Political Force.* We refer to the great Hindu revival under the Mahrattas.

Hindus did not lose their supremacy in Southern India until the empire of Vijayanagar went down before Mussulman invaders at the battle of Talikotta in 1665. A century afterwards, the Hindu peoples of the south—under their heroic leader, Sivaji—threw off the alien yoke, and established the great Mahratta dominion. Sivaji —often described as little better than a bandit— was the first to recognise that India and Hinduism are related organically as body and soul. This makes him the forerunner of Tilak's "new Nationalism"—a fact which is commemorated and made perennially potent by the all-India celebration of Sivaji Day.

The national idea which underlay the Mahratta Empire can be studied in the fascinating pages of Justice Ranade's *Rise and Growth of the Mahratta Power.* Even the most biassed and superficial student of the Mahratta achievement can scarcely fail to recognise that the unity of India was its very soul,—its light and innermost strength. Warren Hastings, whose knowledge of Indian politics was unrivalled, declared (with emphasis) that the Mahrattas were the only people in India who gave evidence of national feeling. Had he lived in the palmy days of Jehangir or Shah Jehan, he would have said (we think) that national sentiment was *universal* in India. But even in his day, the dark time of the eighteenth century anarchy, national sentiment was the secret bond of that great Mahratta's confederacy which included more than half of India.

It is a supremely interesting fact that, even when the Moghul Empire had ceased to wield effective power, there was not a single square inch of the whole area of India that did not acknowledge the sovereignty of the Padshah. Coins were struck and taxes were collected in his name: prayers were offered for him everywhere. Although political power had entirely departed from the descendant of Akbar, the form of universal sovereignty still remained with him. Delhi, his capital, was regarded by all as the unique symbol of India's sacred unity. Tippu alone declared himself independent, and this was as late as 1787, when the Padshah was living in poverty in the palace of his ancestors—his harem outraged, his personal sanctity violated, his power over his personal attendants questioned and defied. Yet we have it on the authority of Sir John Malcolm that Tippu became more unpopular by this one act than by all his cruelty and oppression. On the day after he was slain, Mir Alum, the representative of the Nizam with the British Forces, sought permission from Sir John Malcolm to proceed with an immense concourse to the principal Mosque of Seringapatam in order that he might vindicate the honour of Delhi by reading the State Prayer, in the Padshah's name, in the only place in India in which it had been discontinued.

An even more significant fact is to be found in Mahratta history,—a fact which conclusively proves that, even in the chaotic eighteenth century, Indian statesmen never forgot the unity of India and never ceased to pay homage to the Emperor who symbolised it. The Mahrattas had established a national empire, which was the strongest power in India for a hundred years. Yet they always recognised the sovereignty of Delhi, and when Madhava Rao Sindhia, perhaps the greatest Indian of the eighteenth century, conquered Delhi itself, his first action was to vindicate the insulted majesty of the Moghul Emperor by executing those who had violated his harem. More than this, he publicly paid allegiance to the old monarch, the monarch who was actually his prisoner. The conqueror knelt before the conquered, the Western historian would say: we would be more nearly right if we said that the independent ruler of the whole of North India recognised the sacred unity and inviolable sanctity of his beloved Motherland.

Thus we see that, through uncounted centuries,

the political unity of India has persisted with a constancy truly remarkable. Wars and political division notwithstanding, the conception of "India one and indivisible" has always had at least a latent life.

This unity of India has not been merely the ideal of a few thinkers here and there. It has been felt and prayed for by every devout Hindu, expressed in immortal form in literature and art, and realised practically in the social and religious institutions of Hinduism.

To-day, its life is not latent but active. It makes the Indian peoples *one* people, and because they apprehend it politically, they are not merely a people but a *nation*.[1]

The principle of nationalities is not the ultimate thing that many take it to be, yet the right of self-determination which has been inferred from it is a primary right. To-day the people in India possess that right in its complete form.

[1] See Appendix II.

CHAPTER II

THE ORIGINS AND CAUSES OF THE NATIONAL MOVEMENT

I. Religious Movements

It would be untrue to say that the National Movement in India is distinctively a religious movement, yet no one can study the Movement without remarking its intimate and wide connection with those great religious revivals which have been the salient characteristic of Hindu life during the last five-and-twenty years. English observers have noticed the connection, though not all of them have understood it.

The connection runs back to the very beginning of the National Movement. Nevertheless, the first leaders of Indian Nationalism and the founders of the Indian Congress were outside of it. Those men were a living paradox,—they were denationalised patriots. When the first Congress met, its President—W. C. Banerjea—was looking forward to a political career in England, and Dadābhai Naoroji—who afterwards became a Member of Parliament—was pondering English rather than Indian thoughts.

In this there is nothing to surprise one. A little while ago the very able pen of Sir Valentine Chirol described to us the India of the middle seventies,—the India that he first knew. In those days, says Sir Valentine, the educated young Hindu was apt to be—at least in matters intellectual—*Plus royaliste que le roy.* He had altogether abjured, or had learnt secretly to despise, the beliefs and customs of his forefathers. He respected and admired Englishmen and their life.

On the whole, the picture is faithful. Education of a Western kind had largely de-nationalised—as, perhaps, it was intended to do—those whom it had touched. When India's political mind awoke from its long sleep, it awoke into English Radicalism of the Mid-Victorian sort. That was the creed—nay, it was the *faith*—of the pioneer generations, of the generations represented by Dadabhai Naoroji, Mahadvi Govind Ranade and Gopal Krishna Gokhala.

The first leaders of the National Movement were Indian by birth, but they had abjured most of the things which their fathers had prized,—all that complex tradition which had been aforetime the very soul of their people, and was about to catch a new life from that people's new birth. Those leaders no longer had root in their native soil; they were parasitic upon the West. Their religion was that of Spenser and Comte, their philosophy that of Bentham and the Mills, their tradition that of Macaulay and Jowett. They were *déracinés*.

There was a hidden life in India which felt this like a challenge, and, in the work of two remarkable men, it became an answer and a corrective energy. The religious revival, brought about by Dayananda Saraswati and Swami Vivekānanda, was India's first modern effort for self-protection, her first reply to the challenge of Western culture. From that time onwards an indivisible Nationalism had two aspects,—the one political, the other religious.

To-day India is looking forward to an equal place in the greatest Commonwealth on earth, but in what guise did she appear to her sons—to those who still thought upon her—during the first years of the Empire's rule? A discrowned queen, a neglected mother, that is what they saw.

They felt—and their feeling did not mislead them—that political salvation could come to their land only from a revival of that in it which was most nearly national—*religion.*

The first movement of religious revival under the Empire called itself the Brahma Somaj. That movement was purely religious, it had neither a political message nor a political aim. Therefore, its contribution to Indian Nationalism was, and could be, only an indirect contribution. Nevertheless, the National Movement owes to it a large debt, for it gave to that movement eminent leaders. The founders of the Brahma Somaj, however, were men of the Western culture, and—on the whole—the movement was an Anglicising one. Perhaps this was unintended, but it made the movement unpopular. The Brahma Somaj continued to be a potent religious force in relatively small circles, mostly in Bengal, but as a factor in Indian Nationalism it soon became secondary to a movement plainly and distinctively *National*—the movement of which Sri Ramakrishna was the prophet and Swami Vivekānanda the best expounder.

Those men were Vedāntists. Their religious orthodoxy was informed—perhaps one may add "sustained"—by a profound National sentiment. As it glowed on the eloquent lips of Swami Vivekānanda, Vedāntism was more than a philosophy, it was a *life*—the best and greatest life.

Be that presentation true or false, one thing is quite certain,—the new Vedāntism powerfully counteracted the de-nationalising tendencies of the Missionary and Government schools. Yet no more than the Brahma Somaj had it a political ideal. It was a political force, not through a political message,—it had no such message,—but through its vivid religious nationalism.

A political ideal first became evident in Hinduism when the *Ārya Somaj* became a power in the land. That movement was also a reforming movement,—a movement for a reform in religion. Its founder was a Gujarati Brahmin who—another Buddha—

rebelled against the hide-bound Hinduism which surrounded him. It seemed to him that the *caste system*, founded as it was upon racial and vocational differences, was the very *radix malorum*, the root of the evils that afflicted modern India. This conviction defined for him his life-work. He saw in caste the chief buttress of a vast obscurantism which impoverished life and inhibited growth. Like Nanak the Sikh, he gave himself up to a lifelong effort against it. Yet he did not do what the leaders of the Brahma Somaj had done—he did not break with the religious tradition of his people. Rather did he go back to its first sources and original forms. He appealed to Antiquity,—from the debased and deadening things around him to the simpler, and (as he thought) purer, religion of the Vedas.

The Society which he founded—the Ārya Somaj—became the most important religious organisation in the Punjab. In it, orthodoxy became missionary,—some would say aggressive. The Ārya Somaj set itself to counteract the education given in the Government and Christian schools: to every part of India it sent forth evangelists who preached a new gospel—the gospel of Ārya civilisation. They preached that gospel with fervour, as the hope of India. To the dominant national sentiment of their people they set forth a new social ideal,—one radically and thoroughly Indian.

The political effect of this work was immense.

In Northern India the Ārya Somaj became identified with National Patriotism. Passionate love for the Indian Motherland, tireless and unselfish devotion to the National cause in every field of work,—in education, in social service, in politics, in industrial regeneration,—these were "the fruits of the spirit" in the Ārya Somaj. In it, religion and politics were aspects of one indivisible faith, of one indivisible energy.

This revival of Hindu religion was essentially conservative; it called men back into the ancient ways. True, it made those ways paths of progress, but the progress it envisaged was growth from an ancient root, the development of an old tradition. Not by appropriation of novelties, but by fidelity to a Past perduring in a great inheritance,—thus was India to be saved. That was the gospel of Ārya civilisation.

Stare super antiquas vias—in vernacular words that cry went through the length and breadth of India. It called men to a new kind of life, but it made them intensely conservative.

Conservatism in religion, however, does not always connote conservatism in politics. Anatole France has portrayed for us a philosopher who said something like this: "In all that concerns this world I am a revolutionary. But where the next world is concerned I am a conservative,—nay, a reactionary." We have seen the same thing in India. Some of our most revolutionary politicians have been the most conservative in religion. This has astonished English observers, but the explanation of it is quite simple.

Suppose four things:

1. A foreign government.
2. The absence of political freedom.
3. Potent foreign agencies that de-nationalise.
4. A conservative revival of a national religious tradition.

Is it not clear that the more intense the conservatism of a patriot's revived religion, the stronger will be his reaction against foreign things in politics?

Patriotism, men say, is love of country. So it is, but the Motherland of a Patriot's love is an unseen country,—a home intangible, wherein a great tradition is perpetually renewed. Not in possessed acres, but in an inherited tradition, *there* is the motive and *there* the terms of Patriotism. The more that tradition informs the heart and mind, the more will these reject things alien to it. The stronger the love it evokes unto itself, the stronger will be the antipathy it motives.

No: there is nothing that should surprise us when a conservative religion and revolutionary politics appear as complementary phases of one life.

II. Education

In India, English education has had a tendency to de-nationalise. Some of the first efforts of India's renascent life were efforts of self-protection against it. Nevertheless, it is one of the origins of Indian Nationalism, and—directly or indirectly—it has played a noteworthy part in the development and diffusion of Nationalism.

English education opened up to "Young India" that marvellous autobiography of Freedom—the history of England. It gave to "Young India" Whig spectacles, no doubt, but these made the panorama all the more impressive. From the Witenagemots to the Reform Bill,—it was a wonderful story made splendid by immortal greatness. And "Young India" listened and believed. It believed in the Whig apotheosis of England: it believed that the letters of England's name spelt Freedom everywhere.

The Whig version of England's great political achievement passed into Indian Nationalism. Nothing in the early days of Indian Nationalism is more remarkable than its dependence upon English sources. Its arguments were inferences from what it believed to be England's own faith, its illustrations were emblazoned figures in the Whig roll of honour. The clauses of Magna Carta, the speeches of Hampden, the judgments of Denman were quoted to prove that England should and would impart unto India the English forms of Freedom.

The schoolboy vision passed away, and with it departed the faith—somewhat *naïve*—which it had engendered. This did not happen in a moment. It took five-and-twenty years of disappointment to destroy the splendid Whig panorama. Were the panorama re-presented to-day—were the Ministry of Information to send it to India on a film[1]—it would be received—how? At the best, with courtesy.

Must we say, then, that Indian Nationalism has passed from faith to mistrust? Perhaps not: in these matters, as in others, what looks like logic may be quite misleading. Certain it is, however, that "Young India" has passed through a disillusioning experience. It has discovered—perhaps we are minimising,—that the English tradition of Freedom is more complex than it seemed to be in the Whig version of it.

And there are other things—things of which the tendency is at least agnostic. We will mention two:

(1) Freedom is not prized in England to-day as it was aforetime. This is largely a result of a heterogeneous moral lassitude, but it is also a milestone,—a mark of England's ill-considered (or unconsidered) progress towards the complete form of that un-English thing—the "Modern State."

[1] These words were written in the summer of 1918.

(2) Within our own time, world-wide movements—far from simple—have given to the policies of States a novel national separateness. The States of to-day have a vivid *self*-consciousness, but scarcely any *social* consciousness. The Commonwealth of States does not exist, except in certain much-talked-of possibilities.

England has not remained unaffected by these particularising movements, and—be they good or bad—it can hardly be doubted that they have changed her outlook and somewhat altered her scale of values. The Whig tradition is no safe guide to present-day England.

What should one say to all this? If these things would not justify mistrust, they explain uncertainty and hesitation.

In the year 1813 Sir John Malcolm—the greatest Anglo-Indian of his time—told a Committee of the House of Commons that it would be something like suicide were the British Government to increase the facilities for education in India. Years afterwards, Macaulay recorded a statesman's prevision in these two questions:

"Do you think we can give Indians knowledge without awakening their ambition? Do you think we can awaken their ambition without giving some legitimate vent for it?"

The men who gave to India English education knew what they were doing. They knew that they were preparing, for some future day, changes or discontent. They were brave enough, and great enough, to go on with their work.

That work of theirs became, both directly and indirectly, a primary cause of Indian Nationalism. It gave to India the Whig vision of England: its de-nationalising tendencies motived the religious reaction.

III. Miscellaneous

Under this heading we will not do more than mention three things.

In India it is widely felt and widely believed:

(1) That the military charges upon India are not only out of all proportion to her local needs, but also out of all proportion to her duty in the Empire.

(2) That British predominance in the Administration is, to a considerable extent, an unnecessary drain upon the resources of India.

(3) That the industrial interests of India—so far from being safe in England's keeping—have more than once been sacrificed by England, either to some favourite theory or to industrial interests of its own.

IV. Government and Administration

Indian Nationalism demands for the Indian people two chief things:

(1) Political power.

(2) An "open door" in the Civil Service.

Each of these demands indicates a causal discontent. We will take the second demand first.

A. The average Englishman knows nothing of the Indian Civil Service. He believes it to be excellent because journalists and politicians, officials and globe-trotters, have told him that it is excellent.[1] When one tries to discuss with him reform of the Indian Civil Service, one is nearly always hampered by an inveterate prejudice,—a prejudice which well-nigh makes criticism a hybrid of petty treason and blasphemy.

Well—we take our courage in both hands, and propound three propositions:

(1) That the Indian Civil Service does not command the respect of Indians to the extent that it once did.

(2) It is not as closely in touch with Indian life as it was a generation or so ago.

(3) It is not quite competent to govern India.

At one time, slowness of communication with

[1] He believes the same thing—less confidently and with less justification—of his own Civil Service.

headquarters left much local freedom in the Civil Service—"the man on the spot" had to act for himself. The conquest of Time and Space by the physical sciences, however, has compacted the official machine to such an extent that "the man on the spot" has become little more than a clerk to the man at headquarters.

We are not concerned to deny that England sends to India good clerks, but "good clerks" are not the stuff that statesmen and first-class administrators are made of, and it is *these* that are imperatively required for the highest grades in the Indian Civil Service.

This requirement does not wholly arise out of facts peculiarly Indian. Everywhere administration is part of government and everywhere government is essentially political. Always have men rightly deemed *tact* a prime requisite in administration, but the tact needed to-day is a much greater thing than the tact which sufficed yesterday. *Then* it was merely tact such as made smooth one's everyday intercourse with individuals. *Now* it involves an appreciation of collective thoughts, social forces, political energies and tendencies, and not of these alone, but also of vague moods and unvocal feelings which are always facts *for* Politics, and may (at any moment) become facts *in* Politics. The old-world distinction between things political and things executive has been, to a large extent, obliterated.

Moreover, every large Civil Service has an

advisory as well as an executive function, and for this function no expertness in matters merely executive can suffice. Everywhere and every day the State is preparing for work that will touch the lives of men widely, diversely, intimately, profoundly. The preparation is largely an adjustment—an adjustment of the intended work to a foreseen social and political situation which in some cases is highly and delicately complex. All such pre-adjustment is an essay in statesmanship: an advisory part therein—what is that? That also is a piece of statesmanship.

We are permitted to quote a few words from the report of a Royal Commission—more precisely, from the Reservation which Mr Arthur Boutwood appended to the Majority Report of the Macdonnell Commission on the English Civil Service:

> "8. The work of the Administrative Grade in the Civil Service is a form of political government. Consequently it cannot be performed without high qualities of mind and character. An insight which can thoroughly analyse complex movements in social life, a sympathetic understanding of contemporary tendencies and of the needs and aspirations of men, knowledge that can place facts in their true relation, sound judgment, initiative, tact, courtesy, manliness that can assume and bear responsibility,—these are characteristics of the first-class

> administrator, these are some of the qualities necessary for the higher work of the Civil Service."[1]

Every word of this would still be true were it made part of a Report on the Indian Civil Service, and our primary criticism of that Service is *this*—it is not equal to the higher part of its work. Even its most recent apologist[2] doubts whether it is "calculated to stimulate that part of political talent which consists in the study and guidance of political opinion, and in the framing of large legislative proposals."

It is quite certain that Mr Fisher's doubt is well founded. As for ourselves—we entertain a large doubt.

To be quite frank,—not a few of the men sent out to govern India are men of the wrong type.

We trust that we have cleared the ground sufficiently.

Indians ask for an "open door" in the Civil Service of India. Refusal of this has made many a Nationalist, for,—if the refusal be not merely selfish,—it presupposes one or both of these two things:

(*a*) Indians are unfit for the "open door."

(*b*) The Government does not want the Indian point of view—that point of view *unmediated*—in the higher administration of India.

[1] *Vide* Appendix III.

[2] Mr H. A. L. Fisher, now President of the Board of Education.

B. There is a closed door in the *Administration* of India; there is a closed door in the *Government* of India also. The one excludes Indians from the most important places in the official hierarchy: the other excludes the people of India from political power. Each is a cause of Nationalism, and, of these two causes, the latter—the closed door in the Government—is the more penetrating, and the more widely operative.

The political development which is normal for the State may be described as a process of *moralisation.* It establishes between the Government and the people vital and institutional relations of such a kind that the Government gradually ceases to be a mere *power imposed*—imposed upon the people—and gradually becomes a normative organ of the people's life. It can hardly be said that any development of this kind has taken place in the Government of India. It began as a *power imposed,* and what it was in the beginning that it is now,—perhaps not wholly, but in all forms of political authority, in all the chief energies of political power. In a sense, it is *normative* for the people of India, but it is not *an organ of their life,* and the norms it uses are not expressions of their life. The Government of India is an anachronism.

In fact, if not in theory, the Secretary of State for India is the head—the " head-centre "—of the

Government of India. He is assisted by a Council, and is said to be responsible to Parliament. His Council—the Council of India—is composed of retired Anglo-Indian officials, some City magnates, and two or three Indian gentlemen of official experience or political reputation. Apart from the Secretary of State, it is merely advisory, and the range of its advisory activity is not very large.

Nevertheless, the Secretary is responsible to Parliament! True, but the well-known and well-meant convention—it has well-nigh become a part of the Constitution—that Indian affairs are outside party politics, has so far minimised the Secretary's responsibility to Parliament that it is scarcely more than a non-effective thing piously pretended. *Solutus legibus*—the seventeenth century saw in those words the very quintessence of tyranny, but were they applied to the Secretary of State for India they would have a passable degree of political precision. In matters Indian, the ordinary and invaluable "Parliamentary check" does not effectively exist. So long as the Secretary of State does not openly endanger India, he can do what seemeth good to him, and when he opes his lips, no dog will bark,—he knows beforehand that no attack will be pushed home. The Secretary is master in his own house? No—in India's.

But the Secretary is not a lonely autocrat,—ruling worlds by his nod,—there is the Council of India? That dignified body of superannuated

Civil Servants and "safe" politicians is appointed by the Secretary. He sometimes uses it as a screen, as

> "Feather-bed 'twixt castle-wall
> And heavy brunt of cannon-ball,"

but he would be much surprised if it claimed to be a check. Sir John Strachey, who served for some time on the Council of India, has given us a glimpse of its impotence. He has shown us:

(1) That, in primary matters of policy—such as the Afghan War, the negotiations with Russia, the annexation of Burma—the Secretary of State can and does act without consulting the Council;

(2) That, when the Council is not consulted, it has no means of obtaining information.

So much for the Secretary and his Council.

Let us now turn from Whitehall to India. There also we have a Chief and a Council. In London there is "The Secretary of State in Council of India": in Delhi or Simla there is "The Governor-General in Council." In each case the constitutional authority seems to be a chief in Council. Behind the verbal identity, however, there is a noteworthy difference. In London the connection between Chief and Council is not much more than a formality: in Delhi and Simla it is a very real thing.

In ordinary cases the decisions put forth in the name of "The Governor-General in Council" have, in fact, been taken in Council. When a matter has an urgency quite extraordinary, the Governor-General can, it is true, act without his Council, and, when either the safety or the tranquillity of India is involved, he can override his Council; but even when he exceptionally overrides or exceptionally acts alone, his decision has legal authority only as an Act of "The Governor-General in Council," and as such is it put forth. In India, the supreme local Government is "a Committee Government."

"The supreme local Government"—the designation is unusual, but it has a useful precision. What is called "the Government of India" is subordinate to the Secretary of State. Whenever it pleases the Secretary to give orders to "the Government of India," he expects obedience, and —if there be hesitation or dissent—he is not slow to require obedience. The Duke of Argyll, writing as Secretary of State for India, told Sir John Lawrence—then Viceroy—that the Government of India is an agent of the Secretary of State. He went on to say, "The one great principle that underlies the whole system of imperial administration is that the final control and direction of the affairs of India must rest with the Home Government." Three or four years afterwards, the Marquess of Salisbury repeated this in other words. In effect he told the Government of India that it was bound by his decision—that the Council must vote in accordance with his decision. The published correspondence relating to the resignation of Lord Curzon is conclusive evidence that the Cæsarean prerogatives thus plainly asserted in Whitehall are far from being mere words.

The supreme local Government is subordinate to the Secretary of State: to it are subordinate the Provincial Governments.

Do not suppose that the subordination of the Provincial Governments is limited to matters of political principle; it extends to matters which are purely matters of local administration. In a Memorandum submitted to the Decentralisation Commission, the Bombay Government asserts that the financial arrangements subsisting between the Government of India and the Provincial Governments *tend* to reduce, and—to an extent not inconsiderable—*have* reduced, the Provincial Governments to so many non-entities.

The subordination of the Provincial Governments was not always so extensive,—it is a thing that has gradually increased. The Bombay Government examined the process of extension,—the "increasing purpose" of the Government of India. It could find therein no governing principle, and declared that there seemed to be (in practice) no limit to the control which the Government of India felt empowered to exercise over the Provincial Governments. The migratory Secretariats around the Governor-General have so extravagantly magnified their office that, in many a provincial matter, they have practically ousted the Provincial Government. Nothing is too small for their condescension, nothing too provincial for their capitular magnanimity!

What those migratory Secretariats have done to the Provincial Governments, each Provincial Government has done to its own district officers.

That is how India is governed. There is no longer a Grand Moghul at Delhi—there is one in Whitehall. Under him—moved (when he so desires) by his libertine will,—there is a vast official machine, and (in that wondrous contrivance) each higher wheel, not content with doing its own piece of work, tends to swallow the wheel below it,—and not infrequently succeeds!

Indians, however, have not become Nationalists because the Government of India is over-centralised: they are Nationalists because the political power of the Government of India is not informed with the mind of India.

The Constitution makes all the political power in the Empire the power of the Crown. In England and the Great Dominions, the power of the Crown is institutionally connected with the people in such a way that—in ordinary circumstances—the exercised power of the Crown is the will of the people. In India there is no such constitutional connection. When all is said and done, the people of India are *subjects*,—and nothing more. The political power which they have to obey comes to them *ab extra*—it is outside their life and independent of their will. The Government of India is a power *imposed.* It was *that* when Lord Morley began his beneficent reforms: it was *that* when he finished his work. The changes he made were ameliorations, not remedies. He found the Indian people mere subjects,—he left them mere subjects. True, here and there he gave them a voice, but the cardinal anachronism,—the radical fact which (more than anything else) makes the Government of India a cause of Nationalism,—he left untouched. To-day "the political power of the Government of India is not institutionally informed by the mind of India."

A people that has grown into a national consciousness has a right to political self-determination—that is the primary postulate of Indian Nationalism. To-day, few would deny this postulate,—so few, that to prove it would be a work of supererogation.

The existing subjection of the Indian people has, however, a rarely-pondered consequence which may not be passed over in silence. *It tends to induce servility.*

Mr G. K. Gokhale told the Royal Commission on Public Expenditure that the nature and constitution of India's Government had been a cause of an infinitely great moral evil:

"A kind of dwarfing or stunting of the Indian race is going on under the present system. We must live all the days of our life in an atmosphere of inferiority, and the tallest of us must bend in order that the exigencies of the system may be satisfied."

This conviction — the conviction that British rule has caused a moral deterioration in the national character — is met with at every turn in Indian thought, and has been one of the chief factors in the growth of an aggressive Indian Nationalism.

From the English history which had been taught to them, Indians had gathered that "the meteor flag of England" could not fly in an un-free air,— they thought British Government meant free institutions. Yet they found themselves subject to a British Government that set its face against free institutions! It is not surprising that the first leaders of the National Congress found this a stumbling-block. They could not understand it, —it could not consist with their pathetic confidence that Englishmen loved Freedom for her own sake.

There lies before us the report of a speech made at the second National Congress in 1886, by Pandit Madan Mohun Malaviya. No such speech could be made in India now. As one reads it, one feels that the speaker breathed an air which is not to-day's, and lived by thoughts which are not to-day's. This is what the Pandit said:

"It is not to the great British Government

that we should demonstrate the utility, the expediency, the necessity of representative institutions: it is surely unnecessary to say one word in support of such a cause to the British nation—the descendants of those brave and great men who fought and died to obtain for themselves, and to preserve intact for their children, these very institutions which, taught by their example, we now crave.

What is an Englishman without representative institutions? Why, not an Englishman at all, a mere sham, a base imitation, and I often wonder, when I look round our nominally English Magnates, how they have the face to call themselves Englishmen, and yet deny us representative institutions, and struggle to maintain despotic ones. Representative institutions are as much a part of the true Briton as his language and literature."

The non-representative character of the Indian Government,—its refusal to inform itself with the mind of India,—and the consequent deteriorating subjection of the Indian peoples, have been principal factors in the growth of Indian Nationalism.

No efficient government, no "good government," can be a substitute for that invigorating political right which has been withheld from the people of India.

The National Movement intends an "open door" in the government of India.

CHAPTER III

THE NATIONAL CONGRESS

In the last chapter we set forth origins and causes: we now turn to nature and aims. These—the nature and aims of the National Movement in India—are most clearly apparent in the chief and most conspicuous *organ* of the Movement—the National Congress.

The Indian National Congress was founded at Bombay in the year 1885. Its origins were British, not Indian. It became an organ of militant Nationalism, but this function was unintended, unforeseen, deplored.

The men who first thought of holding an Indian National Congress were certain patriotic Englishmen who were reasonably disturbed by what they saw around them,—by the increasing "unrest" of the "masses" of India, by the increasing alienation of educated Indians from the Government of India. Moved by their reflections, Lord Dufferin—then Viceroy—suggested to a retired Anglo-Indian official the convening of a Congress. He hoped it would be a safety-valve for the British Raj.

The Viceroy's suggestion was acted upon. When

the Congress assembled, however, it took a line which carried it far away from the Viceroy's hopes. This made it seem to Anglo-Indians a seditious body that intended only disaffection. All its official sponsors—except Mr A. O. Hume—were prompt to disavow it.

A

When Indian Nationalists look back upon that first National Congress, they discern in it scarcely anything that would to-day be called Nationalist. True, it advanced political claims on behalf of the Indian people, but the partially-free India it envisaged was not an *Indian* India. The leaders of the Congress were men of the Western culture,—they were dominated by Western ideals. That the West was superior to the East—superior in *kind*—was accepted without question, and some of the most potent minds were convinced (and did not hide their conviction) that, only when India had Europeanised herself, would she be able to take the place which their patriotism defined for her in the community of nations. In effect, they called upon India to cast off her own civilisation and assume another. The chief topic at the Congress was not political enfranchisement, but "Social Reform." The reforms intended were Western, and the plans most discussed were plans for a Western readjustment of India's life. The greatest Indian of the time—Mahadeva Govinda Ranade—was prominent in this work. Mistrust of all things Indian was general and salient. Indeed, it is not too much to say that the sessions of the first Indian National Congress marked one of the most momentous crises in the history of Indian civilisation.

We have already mentioned the de-nationalising effects of the Government system of education. Those effects were intended, and the intention was avowed. The declared intention of the Macaulay Committee was nothing less than this: to cut "Young India" loose from its social moorings, to detach it from the Indian tradition and implant it in another. The eminent Whig historian and his colleagues thought that the whole fabric of Hinduism would fall like a house of cards if only the rising generation could be made to read Newton and Pascal! Those distinguished men were convinced that a generation educated on their plan would turn aside, with a feeling of complacent superiority, from the dramas of Kàlidāsa and Bhavabhūti and take to Shakespeare and Corneille. Macaulay thought that his famous shelf of books—the shelf that he scornfully pretended as the equal of all that had been written in Sanskrit and Arabic—would create in the Indian a contempt akin to his own for the Hindu race and its achievement. And we are compelled to admit that he was not wholly wrong. Some of the most prominent figures at the first

Indian National Congress were "Englishmen of a darker colour,"—Indian only in name,—and the political ideals which guided and inspired that Congress came, not from India, but from Europe. The India of the eighties had lost her native soul. Her first National Congress reflected, not a native faith, but thc setting-sun of a foreign cult,—Gladstonian Liberalism. The lofty thought of John Stuart Mill, Mr Gladstone's life-long work for Freedom,—which then secmed to be culminating in a splendid effort for Ireland,—the new proof of the sufficiency of constitutionalism which was temerariously inferred from the apparent success of the Home Rule campaign—*that* was the inspiration and *these* the encouragement of the Indians who spoke for India in 1885.

Nevertheless, to Indian Nationalists those meetings in Bombay seem epoch-making. In the mere convening of a National Congress they discern an implied recognition—the first modern recognition—of India's political unity, and the spontaneous determination of the Congress to "Social Reform" seems eloquent testimony to the truth of their conviction that India's regeneration must bc the work of her political unity.

What did Anglo-Indians think of the Congress? They were not unanimous, but,—whether in England or in India,—they were all adverse. The less unsympathetic deplored that Indians had turned aside from *la grande affaire* of safeguarding the *status quo.* They had not yet discovered the fact which is the very root of the Indian problem, —the fact that India's life rests upon assumptions which *cannot consist* with those which are fundamental in England's life.

To tell the truth, there was a certain narrowness in England's mid-Victorian *Aufklärung.* Even generous-minded men could conceive of progress only as a development in and through an industrial civilisation. "The brooding East" has apprehended Life quite differently.

What shall we say of the Anglo-Indians who were the more unsympathetic? On the whole, they could see in the Congress nothing but sedition. For the best of them, the *status quo* in India was a sacred inheritance which could not be impaired without sin. Others were mere precursors of the lower Kipling.

Every Anglo-Indian—whatever the degree of his "unsympathy"—perceived quite clearly the danger of an "All-India" National Movement, and every Anglo-Indian fastened upon one and the same prevention. They fastened upon *differences,* and especially upon *two*:

(1) The difference between Hindu and Mohammedan,—which, from the top to the bottom of the social fabric, seemed a cleft that could not be closed; and

(2) upon the difference—much less extensive and

much less conspicuous — between the educated classes and the bulk of the landowners. In the mind of "Anglo-India," differences in India's life—and chiefly the two we have mentioned—became the safety of the British Raj. "Anglo-India" remembered the much-accredited precept, *Divide et impera,* and its recollection became an unobtrusive motive in public policy,—in a policy which was so far successful that it prevented common political action until 1917. Not until the January of that year was there anything like a political union of the two great Indian communities,—the Hindu and the Mahommedan.

At first the Indian Muslims played into the hands of "Anglo-India." It was nothing less than a triumph for "Anglo-India" when Sir Sayed Ahmed—the *princeps* of Indian Mahommedanism—made his famous declaration that the future of his community would be best safeguarded by aloofness from the National Movement.

The defection of Sir Sayed Ahmed might easily have become fatal. Fortunately, the leaders of the Congress Movement discerned the one chance of safety and were bold enough to seize it. They insistently asserted that the Congress was genuinely *national*—the organ, not of a sectional Nationalism, but of Indian Nationalism *as a whole.* In the very darkest days, when most of the Indian Muslims were aberrant in separatism, these men neither wavered nor blenched. They held fast to what seemed to them (and proved to be) the truth that the differences in India are *differences within a political unity,* and they preserved for that unity an institution apt to be its organ. Their faith was great and their achievement notable.

B

Not until the end of the nineteenth century did the National Congress approximate to what is now called "aggressive Nationalism." The earlier Presidential Addresses defined modest aims, and opened up a very limited prospect. A larger share in administration, the gradual introduction of a representative element into the provincial Legislative Councils,—these small things were the boons for which the leaders of Indian Nationalism then pleaded, in earnest words of much eloquence. In those early Congresses there was no general demand either for integral self-government,—the self-government we have in mind when we speak of "the self-determination of peoples,"—or for any large measure of self-government. As yet, the Congress had scarcely caught a glimpse of that "free India" which is at once the term, the norm, the inspiration of to-day's Nationalism.

No: in those days Indian Nationalism was far from being "aggressive." There was truth in the untrue gibe that the Indian agitator would be content to live under the Government he publicly execrated, if only it would make him an "Honourable."

Well, it is easy to jeer, and men born of a great

tradition—which had garnered the political experience of unique centuries—were not slow to jeer at the political *in*experience of those Indian postulants. Of course they were inexperienced. Under British rule, as it then was, they could hardly be anything else. Yet those inexperienced men accomplished a great work of political education. Those earlier Congresses—whatever their limitations and defects—trained the men who became the not inexperienced leaders of the next Nationalist generation. From its very beginning the Congress Movement was far from being a mere agitation of non-entities. Some of the most gifted Indians of the day belonged to it. Among the chiefs of the early Congresses were :

Sir Pherose Shah Mehta, whose work on the Municipal Corporation of Bombay has earned for him the undying gratitude of his fellow-countrymen ;

Gopala Krishna Gokhale of Poona, destined to be widely recognised as a far-seeing statesman of no common ability and strict integrity ;

Surendra Nath Bannerjea and Bhupendra Nath Basu, both from Bengal ;

Rajah Sir T. Madhava Rao, who had administered three of the most important Indian states ; and

Sir C. Sankaran Nayar of Madras, now Minister of Education in the Viceroy's Cabinet.

"Men of no political experience,"—one remembers exceptions, but, on the whole, that description, which is a criticism, is true. Yet, of those men without experience, not a few have since become laureate,—some in what is called "public life," others in administrative work. One recalls the names of R. C. Dutt, Sir Satyendra Prasanna Sinha—who has twice been the Indian delegate to the Imperial Conference—and of another whom we have just mentioned,—Sir Sankaran Nayar. Only three? True, but those three are representative. They stand for a number which is not inconsiderable.

As time went on the mood and policy of the Congress changed. At the sessions held during the last years of the nineteenth century, it became clearly evident that a new spirit was at work in India,—that Indian Nationalism was ceasing to be "tame," and was becoming "aggressive."

To some extent this change was a result of happenings outside the Congress Movement. It was the time of the South African War. On the whole, Nationalist India thought of that war as a large part of English Liberalism thought,—to both it seemed an "imperialistic" aggression. That war had far-reaching effects in India.

(1) The course of the war diminished Britain's military *prestige*,—the power behind the British Raj no longer seemed invincible.

(2) The origins of the war—or what were taken

> to be its origins — diminished Britain's political *prestige*. The England of the Whig tradition gave place to another England, and that other England—far from being the very spirit of Freedom in human history—seemed belligerent against Freedom.

Then, India itself was swept by plague and famine, and incidental happenings, which many deemed administrative blunders, created an unrest which spread like wildfire.

All this was reflected in the contemporary sessions of the Congress. Administrative acts were criticised with fierce antagonism, and—for the first time—the attitude of the Congress towards the Government became one of hostility. Tilak's opportunity was close at hand.

For some time Nationalists of the younger generation had been discontented with the Congress. They had been drawn into the Congress Movement by the immense prestige of its first leaders, but (latterly) the political ineffectiveness of the Congress had alienated them. Its eloquence that seemed unmeaning, its faith in words, its party-wrangles,—these things could not satisfy the more thoughtful: its holiday aspect, its unwieldy frame, irritated the more earnest. Discontent soon became open revolt. There were men in the Congress who had lost faith in petitions, resolutions and deputations,—who were not content to leave all initiative to the Government, who would no longer consent to approach the Government as political mendicants or as worshipful suppliants. Their hour had come.

The founding of *New India* in 1901 may be taken as the first public act of these New Nationalists. Their marked intellectual power, their whole-hearted devotion to the Indian Motherland, soon made them the most potent party—from the point of view of the Government, the most formidable party—in Indian public life.

The leader of this new party, the "father" of this New Nationalism, was none other than Bal Gangadhar Tilak. His orthodoxy was unimpeachable, his patriotism beyond question,—before long, he was both idolised and execrated. His personality is a symbol of his Movement, his public career is an epitome of it.

Tilak is a Chitpavan Brahmin from Poona. After taking Honours at Bombay, he threw himself into educational work. He first of all joined the well-known Sarvayanika Sabha of Poona—then controlled by Mahadeva Govinda Ranade—and took an active part in the work of Fergusson College and other educational institutions maintained by that great Society. This work made him for some time the associate of his future opponent, Gokhale,—also a Chitpavan Brahmin. These activities, however, were not sufficient for his enthusiasm. He turned to politics, and, like

Louis Kossuth—to whom, as a political leader, he bears a striking resemblance,—he began his political career with an organised "Press-campaign." The *Kesari* was Tilak's *Pesti Hirlap*, and—until it was suppressed in 1908—this paper was the chief organ of the Nationalist party in the Mahratta country.

Of all the Indian leaders Tilak was the first to recognise that Hindu Nationalism would never become a considerable force until it had ceased to be purely secular,—Hindu Nationalism must be supported by Hindu Orthodoxy. His profound Sanskrit learning, and his strict conservatism in religion, gave him much influence with the Hindu population on the west coast. In the hope of making that influence a political force for the regeneration of India, he founded the Anti-Cow-Killing Society, and this at once became a focus and organ of extreme religious conservatism. In another institution, which bore the famous name of Sivaji,[1] Tilak essayed a piece of work more distinctively political. The establishment of it was an effort to revive the national spirit of the Mahrattas. Sivaji is still a name to conjure with among the martial races of the Deccan, and, with sure political insight, Tilak sought to make the cherished tradition of their splendid past the basis and inspiration of a militant Mahratta Nationalism.

[1] Sivaji is the national hero of the Mahrattas. He put an end to Moghul rule on the west coast, and established in its place a Mahratta *imperium* which lasted until 1818.

Tilak was not left to work single-handed. In the North, Lajpat Rai—unsullied by political ambition, above all party-wrangles—gave to the New Nationalism the weight of his noble personality. His support was the more valuable because he was one of the trusted leaders of the Ārya Somaj—the orthodox and far-extended society which has done so great a work for India. In Calcutta, another orthodox Hindu—Bepin Chandra Pal—gave Tilak the powerful support of that militant paper *New India*.

Lajpat Rai, Bepin Chandra Pal,—these Indians were eminent, and they did much, very much, to further the New Nationalism. But who did most? An Englishman, not eminent but *eminentissimus*—proconsular then, more than proconsular since. Tilak's best recruiting-sergeant was none other than the Viceroy of India—Lord Curzon. His tactlessness made his words heavy with provocation: his narrowness made British Imperialism an affront to Indian sentiment. His reactionary policy in education, his outrageous behaviour to the Calcutta Corporation, his contempt (scarcely veiled) for the men who were doing what they could for India in politics, his mischievous attempt to separate the uneducated many (complacently supposed to be Curzonian) from the educated few (supposed to be sedition-mongers),—these things were enough to make the most lukewarm Nationalist militant. They were deeply felt and hotly resented throughout the length and breadth of India.

Lord Curzon's maladroit policy culminated in the partition of Bengal. A "settled fact," said Lord Morley—yet it has passed out of life into the limbo where blunders are undefended. But, before it passed away, it raised a storm in India which no *Hic jacet* could appease.

Around that blunder a whole literature has grown up. It moved every orator and every journalist in Bengal—and Bengal abounds in both—to passionate outpourings. The storm raged for well-nigh eight years. Then a new reign began graciously, and the partition was undone.

"The partition was undone." True, but the partition of Bengal had been more than a re-arrangement in the administrative machine,—it had been a political force working passionately in millions of hearts, and what it did *there* was not undone.

The partition of Bengal gave to the extreme Nationalists—" the new Party " as they began to style themselves—the tactical opportunity which their chiefs had long desired and long sought. Tilak and his colleagues had seen quite clearly that the New Nationalism would not become what they wished it to become unless they could utilise the organisation which their precursors had built up, and could convert to their uses the magic of that immense personal popularity which those men had acquired by five-and-twenty years of untiring work. The younger generation needed to invest its work with the authority of the elder.

The agitation consequent upon the partition created the longed-for opportunity. Even the political conservatism of Hindustan protested,—even men like the Maharajah of Burdwan and Dr (now Sir) Rash Behari Ghose. Those first protests were in the old tone of supplication, but they had the effect of a tocsin. In a few months India was roused as never before in our time, and the protest which began in prayer culminated in open defiance. The Boycott and Swadeshi—*these* were the New Party's answer to Lord Curzon, and, from the presidential chair of the Benares Congress, *these* were publicly approved by Gokhale himself. The "novelists" had won,—the new had the authority of the old.

While a ruler's maladroitness was driving Indian Nationalism to extremes, events which marked a new epoch in world-history were taking place in Manchuria: Japan was winning the Russo-Japanese War! To the millions of India the victory of Japan seemed a victory of the East over the West,—of Asia over Europe,—and this view of it set up a tidal-wave of feeling which became a new and abiding factor in the Nationalist Movement. It is arguable that Indian Nationalists would not have gone the length they went in 1906 and 1907 had they not been electrified by Japan's victories in 1905.

Turn now to the proceedings of the Congress.

The Congress of 1903 had been remonstrant like its predecessors. It had shown itself adverse to pageant-shows, to Mr Chamberlain's economic Imperialism, and to "the consecrated Goddess of Public Opinion." Signs of the coming storm were already visible, but the general tone of the Congress was mild,—for a time of repression and reaction, very mild. In 1904 the Congress contented itself with an emphatic protest against the partition of Bengal,—then recently proposed.

In the sessions of 1905, however,—these were held at Benares,—it soon became evident, and every one felt, that the Congress had been transformed. Deafening shouts of "Vande Mātaram!"[1] proclaimed to the world that Indian patriotism had ceased to be coquetry and had become a love. No Indian would discount the patriotism of the early Congress-men. It was, however, an intellectual attitude rather than a passionate conviction. It was not "a sovereign dogma"—inflaming the mind, inspiring the heart, informing the imagination. The cry "Vande Mātaram!" testified to a profound change,—one of those momentous changes that create new epochs.

Another thing made the Congress of 1905 a noteworthy one,—the personal ascendancy of the Mahratta leader. Tilak—with whom the New Nationalism is to a large extent bound up—had devoted all his marvellous energy to the

[1] "Vande Mātaram" became the war-cry of the Nationalists. It means "I worship the Mother" or "Hail, Mother."

political amelioration of India. "India a nation!"—no longer a mere dependency, but freely a co-ordinate partner in a British Commonwealth of self-governing States—*that* was the light of his thought, the pole-star of his effort. In the Mahratta country no one was more popular than this modern Sivaji,—no one so venerated, no one so loved. Though his work for the Indian Motherland had been uninterrupted,—save for a period of imprisonment, during which he wrote a masterly treatise on the antiquity of the Vedas,—he had hitherto kept in the background at the annual sessions of the Congress. In the Congress of 1905, however, he was asked to move the important—very important—Resolution on Poverty. Excitement was intense. An ovation, such as no other Congress had witnessed, welcomed this proven champion of orthodoxy in religion and Nationalism in politics. The new Sivaji had come into his kingdom!

During 1905 the New Party gained ground so fast that both the Moderates and the Government were alarmed. There can be no doubt that a gospel of violence was spreading like wildfire. The Government acted vigorously. It suppressed papers, imprisoned editors, deported leaders. So long, however, as the Congress was not openly divided, repression did little more than play the extremists' game. The Moderates dared not stand aside,—they *had* to join in the general protest. So, from the Congress of 1905 there went up to the seats of power, India's univocal shout of condemnation, and Surendra Nath Bannerjea—in the eloquence of a forgotten day—lectured the Government on the efficacy of Freedom as a preventive of sedition and anarchy!

But although united in protest, the Congress was divided in discussion. And the differences were not superficial,—they went down to the foundations of policy. When men looked forward to the Congress of 1906, disruption seemed inevitable. To prevent that imminent disaster, all parties united in calling to the presidential chair the much-esteemed Moderate, Dadabhoi Noaroji,—a Parsi veteran who (twenty years before) had been one of the leaders of the first Congress, and had twice been President of the Congress. What happened? In the Congress of 1906 (held at Calcutta), the President not only approved the primary heads of the New Party's fighting policy—Swadeshi and the Boycott—but he set forth *Swa Raj* ("Self Rule," such as the greater colonies enjoyed), as the ideal of the Congress. From that moment it became clear that the Congress Movement must either pass altogether into the hands of the New Party, or must purge itself of extremists.

During 1907 the tension between the Indian parties increased. Such was the popular enthusiasm for the New Party, that the Moderates felt themselves being driven into a back-water. The Surat Congress of that year—it met at

Christmas-time—was marked by violent scenes and ended in a split. For the next eight years Indian Nationalism was a divided force, and to no small extent its dissociated parties were mutually hostile.

That disruption gave to the British Government an opportunity which it did not neglect. The Cabinet of the day was Liberal, and Lord Morley was a member of it as Secretary of State for India. He was not without experience of Nationalist movements, for he had been Chief Secretary for Ireland under Mr Gladstone. The disruption in India amounted to an invitation. Lord Morley set out to rally the Indian Moderates to the standard of Constitutionalism, and he set up that standard in a Bill which included (in modified forms) most of the things for which the earlier Congress had petitioned. The Bill became an Act.

It seemed a victory for the Moderates and for "constitutional methods." But what moved Lord Morley when he set out to rally the Moderates? Not "constitutional methods,"—certainly not. The Liberal Government permitted Lord Morley to make that adventure *because the popular strength of the New Party had become a menace.* The reforms of 1909 were a direct result of "aggressive Nationalism."

CHAPTER IV

THE NEW PARTY AND ITS TENETS

LORD MORLEY set out to "rally the Moderates." As soon as it became clear that his adventure had succeeded, the Government of India set out to suppress the men who had not rallied. With the approval of Lord Morley, strong repressive action was taken against the leaders and organs of the New Party. It looked as though the Government intended to silence criticism and eradicate opposition. The papers of the New Party were silenced one by one. The *Karma Yogin* ceased to exist, the *Vande Mātaram* was suppressed, the *Punjabee* and the *Hindu* changed hands. All the vernacular papers of the Party were either gagged or rooted out one by one; the leaders of the Party were imprisoned, deported, or exiled. Tilak himself was arrested, and sent to imprisonment at Mandalay, in Burma. Arabindo Goshe, the leader of the New Party in Bengal, was charged with conspiracy, and, though acquitted,—so completely that not a slur remained upon him,—life was made so impossible for him that he left the shelter of the Union Jack, and took refuge with the French in Pondicherry.

Bepin Chandra Pal found Calcutta intolerable, and transferred his work to London.

The New Party was broken, dispersed, and silenced. In India its voice was no longer heard: only from intangible seclusion in Paris or San Francisco—where a few fiery souls became more fiery because they thought themselves safe—came intermittent outbursts, frantic and extravagant, which did the cause of India no good.

"Broken,—dispersed,—silenced"—the passing-bell was tolling, and no *Resurgam* was evident.

The New Party had had a very short life—two years and a half. Yet in that short time it had wrought a revolution in India's political thinking. In 1907, *Swa Raj*—complete Home Rule—was a novel political heresy: to-day, it is one of the commonplaces of public life. In that change the defeated have their victory. Two years and a half!—that "crowded hour of glorious life" brought India nearer to Freedom than a hundred years of constitutional agitation by the Moderates would have done. Two years and a half! What were the thoughts that filled those years with energy? They are worth knowing for their own sake, and also, because, in the work of the Home-Rule-for-India Party, they have become the chief political energy of to-day.

The main difference between the Nationalists and the Moderates in 1907 was well expressed by Tilak in a stirring address which he delivered at Calcutta on the 4th of January 1908. Essentially, it was not the difference between part of a thought and its completeness—it was the difference between a piecemeal policy and an integral policy.

Some—like Gokhale, to whom the British Raj seemed "an inscrutable dispensation of Providence"—believed that India could become politically adult (*sui juris*) only by a long period of slow growth, and they thought British rule necessary in order to protect and foster that growth or (at least) to give time for it. To those who thought thus, Tilak said, "We differ, and cannot co-operate. Let us part as friends." For his own part, he believed that India was fit for immediate self-government, and (consequently) that British rule—which is not the same thing as the British connection—had become vitally harmful.

The Moderates asked—for what did they ask? For "a greater share in the administration of the country." Tilak and his friends asked for Swa Raj,—complete self-government of the Colonial kind—and for that *at once*. They stood, in fact, for the immediate political self-determination of India. Their Nationalism was an *integral* Nationalism. It set forth the National Right in its completeness, and as an *immediate* Right. "Swa Raj at once,"—*that* was their policy.

After all, what did "a greater share in the administration of the country" mean? If it meant nothing but a High Court Judge here, a Member of the Council there, or even if it meant more elected members in the Legislature or a Civil Service entirely Indian,—then, from Tilak's point of view, the achieving or granting of it would not alter, largely or in any vital way, the existing situation. As long as the Government of India was not entirely responsible to the people of India, and to them alone,—as long as it was not uniquely and wholely determined by the mind of India to the needs of India,—the essentials of the harmful *status quo,* the essentials that made it harmful, would continue.

That, at least, is what the Nationalists contended. Against the piecemeal policy of the Moderates, they advanced their *integral* policy,—"Swa Raj at once."

The Nationalists did not suppose that the Government of India would spontaneously transfer to them its powers, rights, and duties. They foresaw that some kind of compulsion would be necessary. What, then, should be done? The Moderates, for the success of their piecemeal policy, trusted to what were designated "constitutional methods,"—public meetings, resolutions, deputations. In fact, they premised that the Government of India could be argued out of its position. They premised this, although they could not show any reason why the Government should condescend to argue at all. They trusted, we may say, to *compulsion by ideas.* The Nationalists, on the other hand, preferred *compulsion by vital forces.* They would have nothing to do with what seemed to them the dull futility of " constitutional agitation." They were fighters, not petitioners—their weapons were Swadeshi and the Boycott. Boycott the Government, Boycott the Courts, Boycott British goods, — in fact, organise a general passive obedience (or passive resistance) which would make administration impossible—*that* was the method by which they hoped to obtain Swa Raj. The vital thing, they said, in the existence of every Government, is *prestige.* Now, Boycott would strike at the very roots of the Government's *prestige.* Therefore—Boycott !

This doctrine was elaborated by Bepin Chandra Pal in those Madras speeches which are still the most authoritative exposition of the new creed and the new method.

He summed up the new programme thus :

> Organise all the resources of the nation, synthesise all its forces. Make the *general* need for Freedom the motive of a *general* integration, at once material and spiritual.

Were that done, the National Movement would become (he thought) a militant vital energy which no Government would be able to withstand.

That is no small conception; yet, when one turns to the means by which it was to be realised, one catches a glimpse of something much larger. The Nationalists had not only a fighting policy, they had also a constructive programme. This programme included four chief things :

(1) The promoting of education.
(2) The raising of national volunteers.
(3) The development of Indian industries.
(4) The establishment of a political organisation intended to assume unto itself as much as possible of the work that had been left to the Government.

From the point of view of political methodology, the fourth of these things was by far the most important. The Nationalists intended a national integration of Indian life and work; but not that alone. Undeterred by the famous writ *Præmunire*,—indeed without thinking about it,—they intended ***an immediate assumption of political power.*** Arabindo Ghose — a young Cambridge graduate who was the philosopher of Integral Nationalism—set this forth quite plainly in an article which was published in *Bande Mātaram* on the 22nd of January 1908:

> "We must devise means of stimulating the activities of our people. This cannot be better done than by organising a really representative assembly, which, in its annual or periodical course of sitting, will decide our course of action. It does not necessarily follow that it will come into collision with the powers that be. . . . Let

us thus relieve the bureaucratic administration of as much of its duties, in as many departments as possible."

Those words were published, as we have said, in 1908. By the end of that year the New Party had ceased to exist; the Moderates, with Gokhale at their head, were in sole possession of the field. But the New Party, though defeated, had done something which could not be *un*done,—not by the seemingly victorious Moderates, not by the Government itself. The New Party had compelled both the Moderates and the Government to declare—*these* what they desired, *that* what it intended, for the future of India.

Most official Anglo-Indians—indeed, all but a very few—had been content to reiterate the doctrine of India's perpetual tutelage—to them a comfortable doctrine, for it confirmed them in their pre-eminence. The earlier Congress leaders, as we have seen, had no clear vision of a political future for India—they respectfully presented to "the present power" a few complaints, and did not see their way to very much more. Neither the official classes nor the Congress leaders were prepared for the New Party's bold demand—"Swa Raj at once!" When it was made it staggered them. A blind drift, guided by an inscrutable Providence,—*that* was the Moderate vision of India's political life. What chance had it against the energy that lived alertly in the new cry, "Swa Raj at once"? They also cried "Swa Raj!"—careful only to preserve their moderation by refusing to add "at once." Even "the Bureaucracy" felt that the times had changed. After much hesitation, it brought itself into line with the Moderates, and declared for the gradual initiation of the Indian peoples into the mysteries of government. The impetus of the New Party had carried things a long step forward. Swa Raj, though diversely accepted, had become a common ideal.

CHAPTER V

THE PRESENT POSITION

BEFORE the recent understanding between the Indian parties, the diversities in India's life were the predominant facts in Indian politics. The Mohammedan would have no political dealings with the Hindus: the landed aristocracy looked askance at the educated *bourgeoisie*.

The New Party was a *Hindu* Party: its brilliant campaign of 1907-08 was wholly the work of educated Hindus. The Mohammedans held aloof. They had been separated from the National Movement—years before—by Sir Sayed Ahmed, and they still saw in the political *status quo* the chief safeguard of their community's future and of their present political importance. They felt that the awakening of India into political self-consciousness would make all things Mohammedan subordinate to things Hindu; they feared, in fact, that a Hindu flood would carry everything before it.

The Government, true to an Imperialism circumscribed by British supremacy, and not perceiving that this had already become a political anachronism, openly favoured the Mohammedans. It hoped thereby:

(1) to convince the Mohammedans that their commercial interests would be safeguarded better by dependence upon the Government than by co-operation with their fellow-countrymen ;

(2) to withhold the Mohammedans from the Congress Movement ; and thus

(3) to make it impossible for the Congress to claim for itself a *national* character.

This policy was far from being unsuccessful. Not only did the Mohammedans abstain from taking any part in the Congress Movement—they organised themselves against it. They founded the All-India Muslim League, and, in its early years, this was a political counterpoise to the Congress, because it testified for Mohammedan "loyalty" against Hindu "sedition," and—by its mere existence—seemed to prove that the Congress which called itself "National" was *not* national, but sectional.

The days of "Divide and Rule," however, were drawing to a close.

The work of the All-India Muslim League, and the various activities incidental to the existence and work of the league, were a political education for the Mohammedans, and, as this education progressed, it changed their outlook. The New Nationalism of 1906 had the support of not a few young Mussulmans. Their leader was the late Abdul Rasul, a young Oxford man whose very promising life was suddenly cut short by heart-failure in 1916. The chief part, however, in disposing the Mussulmans toward co-operation with the Hindus, and in making their patriotism something more than a communal interest, was played by events (outside of India) that set the whole world of Islam a-thinking,—we refer to the revolutionary National Movements in Persia and Turkey.

Prior to the insurgent birth of Nationalism in the two chief Islamic States, Pan-Islamism had been a fashionable cult among the Mussulmans of India. Now, the Pan-Islamic fantasy—its day-dream of a vast Mohammedan Empire extending from the Atlantic to Burma—ignored *nationality*, and presupposed a politico-religious unity which was not national—not even *inter*national—but *supra*-national. Clearly, Nationalism could not consist with it; and when national movements became successful in Turkey and Persia, men were not slow to infer that Pan-Islamism had received a wound likely to become fatal. And so it had, but, before it received that wound, it had shaken the anti-national understanding which subsisted tacitly between the Indian Mussulmans and the Government of India.

The Government of India had made the communal sentiment of its Mohammedan subjects one of the pillars of its policy. That sentiment, however, had "two soul-sides,"—one to face the Hindu world with, one to tell foreign Mussulmans that they had brothers in India. In so far as it separated the Indian Mussulmans from their Hindu fellow-countrymen, it seemed to the Government of India a very fine thing: in so far as it made those Mussulmans consciously part of the general Islamic world, it was well-nigh as abominable as the "seditious" Hindu Congress. So, when the Indian Mussulmans began to talk Pan-Islamism, the Government frowned on them. It was a natural thing for the Government to do, but—those official frowns caused much heart-searching. Men began to feel that the Government would (if it could) exclude the Indian Mussulmans from any life larger than that of an isolated non-political community in India.

It is no wonder that the Indian Mussulmans began to reconsider their position. Their natural outlook included, on the one hand, their Hindu fellow-countrymen, and, on the other, their co-religionists outside India. Their sympathy with the latter had taken a political colour from Pan-Islamism, but—the Government of India had frowned on Pan-Islamism, the national awakening in Turkey and Persia had destroyed the unity which Pan-Islamism presupposed, and the Tripolitan war showed (or seemed to show) that the principal Islamic State was no longer equal to a victorious military effort. The Indian Mussulmans recognised that they had not (and could not have) an international *status* of their own, and they began to perceive that the greatness of their community must be part of the greatness of India.

A rapid change of opinion set in. The Balkan wars made the more advanced members of the Mohammedan community bitterly "anti-English," and they were confirmed in their new attitude by the regrettable experiences that befel Mr Mohammed Ali and Mr Wazir Hassan when those leaders of the new Muslim movement came to England.[1] The deposition of Mr Ameer Ali and the Agha Khan from the leadership of the Muslim League showed that the younger Muslim generation was no longer deterred by the bogey of "Hindu supremacy" which the magic pen of Anglo-Indian journalism—it used a black magic—had conjured up.

This *rapprochement* between the All-India League and the National Congress is the most outstanding and most significant feature of the Indian National Movement at the present time. These two bodies have put forth a common programme[2]; they stood shoulder to shoulder during the momentous agitation which led up to the "Augustan" promise,—the promise made on the 20th of August 1917; they have worked together strenuously (and with mutual loyalty) for the ideal which has become common to them both,—Swa Raj for India. Mohammedans and Hindus have become compatriots, and this vital integration of forces which the Government had hoped to keep separate is a conclusive defeat for the policy

[1] They were interned.

[2] It is known as the Congress-League Scheme.

of "Divide and Rule" on the field where it seemed to have the best chance. The Bureaucracy had hoped that the diversities within India's life would become a perpetuation of its power. The most important of those differences—that between Mohammedans and Hindus—is no longer a political difference. "Mohammedans and Hindus have become compatriots."

And what of the other great difference—that between the educated *bourgeoisie* and the old aristocracy? That also has lost its political importance.

Even in its early days, the Congress contained such men as the Nawab Sayid Mohammad—great-grandson of Haidar Ali, the redoubtable Sultan of Mysore. Those men, however, were exceptional, and their presence in the Congress did but make the more conspicuous the well-nigh general abstention of their class. In those days, the Hindu aristocracy of India had no political education and much apathy. No change in Modern India, however, has been more marked than the change which has come over the ancient aristocracy of the land. The enlightened policy of the Agha Khan—pontiff of the numerous Khoja sect—has earned for him and brought to him a world-wide reputation. The Rajah of Mahammadabad—premier nobleman in Oudh, the Maharajah of Burdwan—the largest landowner in India, and the Rajah of Ramnad, have openly adhered to the National Cause; and what these have done a host of other nobles and landowners have also done.

On the Supreme Legislative Council, the Secretary of the Madras Home Rule League—a pronounced Nationalist—is the elected representative of the Madras landowners, and, on all important occasions, the "landed interest" in that Council has voted with the "popular interest."

The All-India Muslim League and the National Congress have joined forces: the aristocracy no longer stands aloof. These changes are momentous,—what effect have they had on and in the National Movement? Always national in aim, it has now become national in extension. Always invested with the authority of sound political thought, it now has—what, for any such work in India is invaluable and indispensable—the *prestige* of great names and old dignities.

What is the aim of to-day's Nationalism? Unrestricted Home Rule, Swa Raj, complete political self-determination—*that* is the aim, and it is an aim which has created in India a unity which transcends all the differences within India's life.

It should not be supposed, however, that this unity is an undiversified unity. Complete Home Rule? Yes, that is the common aim. But when?

The Non-Brahmin[1] Party of Madras says

[1] This may be called the "Extreme Right" of the National Party.

"Not Now." It fears that "Swa Raj at once" would hand India over to the Brahmins.[1] This party was led by Dr T. M. Nair,—a man of good position, of great and unquestioned ability. Its organ in the Press is a Madras paper called *Justice*. This carries on a vigorous campaign—one directed as much against the Nationalist Centre and Left as against the Brahmins. Indeed, its attack on "Swa Raj *at once*" is pushed so far, and seems so little discriminating, that men have taken it to be an attack upon "Swa Raj at any time," and have supposed the members of the Non-Brahmin Party to be India's Ulstermen.

Now—this cannot be said too plainly—the Non-Brahmin Party is a *Nationalist* Party. It accepts the common aim, Swa Raj, but differentiates itself by an idiosyncrasy which it makes a policy. It opposes "Swa Raj at once" because it thinks Swa Raj at once would mean government by a much-privileged caste,—the Brahmins,—and because it thinks government of that kind would confirm and tend to perpetuate a harmful thing that should be broken down—to wit, the caste system.

It is, however, very far from being on the side of the Bureaucracy. It stands, in fact, for "Federal Home Rule *gradually*."

"It is impossible," says Dr Nair, "to devise a satisfactory scheme of self-government for India

[1] This will remind English readers of a cry which, a few years ago, had some vogue in England,—"Home Rule means Rome Rule."

except on the basis of Federal Home Rule, and in any scheme of Federal Home Rule the units of the system should be properly constituted before we can think of constituting the federal authority."

All this is quite clear. The Non-Brahmin Party is a *Nationalist* Party,—differentiated by its preference for a federal constitution and a gradual method. The clouds of dust raised by its forcible and incessant attacks upon "Swa Raj at once" have hidden from English eyes its large agreement with the rest of the Nationalist Party; but in India—in Indian India—that agreement, and the extent of it, are well known. Brahmins and non-Brahmins are agreed that India should have complete provincial autonomy, that Indian industries should be fostered, that the Government's railway policy should be modified, and—last, but not least—that a general system of primary education for the masses should be established forthwith.

Outside the Non-Brahmin Party—which is pledged to Swa Raj—there is little organised *Indian* opposition to "Swa Raj *at once*."

The Moderate Party? No doubt there are still Moderates in India, but it can hardly be said that there is still a Moderate Party. A few Indians have not yet forgotten the Whig version of England's history. This still keeps alive in them an obsolete faith, and they continue to expect, from England's magnanimity, some spontaneous gift of self-government. Moderates of this kind are prominent figures in the City of Bombay and among the aristocracy of Madras and Bengal. Their influence, however, is no longer what it was—chiefly because their policy lost its brains when Pherose Shah Mehta and Gokhale died.

Lord Morley, as we have seen, set out to "rally the Moderates," and he succeeded. His success seemed to infer victory to the Moderates—in reality it prepared the way for their downfall. One by one their leaders accepted office and dropped out of the national movement. Thus were Sir S. P. Sinha, B. N. Basu, Sir C. Sankaran Nayar and Sir Ibrahim Rahimtoolla lost, and the places they left vacant have not been filled. Deprived of their leaders, the Moderates could not understand the increasingly forceful attacks of the men who were not "Moderate," and to-day,—whatever their number,—their influence, outside official circles, is inconsiderable. Not only have they lost the Congress, which had almost become their private domain, but (one by one) the daily papers have fallen away from them,—to Integral Nationalism, to Home Rule. To their lost cause, names which are justly revered still give an impotent dignity: Surendra Nath Bannerjea—at one time the uncrowned King of Bengal—and Sir Dinshaw E. Wacha still try to make "constitutional agitation and steady progress" a rallying-cry;

but the day of the Moderates is over, there is no longer a Moderate Party.

We have mentioned Tilak's imprisonment in Mandalay. He was liberated in July 1914, and at once resumed his political work. His party—the party of religious Nationalism—instantly revived. But the Great War broke out, and the fervent loyalty of the Indian peoples threw everything else into the background.

Soon after the outbreak of the War, Mrs Besant became associated with Tilak. Some time before, after a varied public life in England, Mrs Besant had come to India as a leader of what seemed to Indians a conservative religious movement—that is to say, as a leader of the Theosophical Society. At first she held herself entirely aloof from Indian politics. This attitude, however, could scarcely be permanent,—her religious propaganda and her work for national education were bound, sooner or later, to bring her into the current of the National Movement.

A month before the war broke out, Mrs Besant began to interest herself in the political movements around her, and her well-earned influence helped to gain for the national cause many men of considerable standing in commerce and industry. At first Mrs Besant was associated with Gokhale—the eminent Moderate. While he and Sir Pherose Shah Mehta lived, the methods of Integral Nationalism did not have much success, although the reappearance of Tilak had brought back to that policy much of the activity and enthusiasm which had carried it forward so brilliantly in 1907 and 1908. Those two leaders, however, both died in 1915, and for the Moderates that loss spelt defeat. Tilak took Gokhale's place with Mrs Besant, and under his influence she became a violent Home Ruler.[1]

It soon became evident what the Moderates had lost by the death of their veteran leaders—both men of outstanding ability. The Congress of 1915 virtually adopted the Home Rule programme of Tilak and Mrs Besant. The next Congress—that of December 1916—was openly extremist. It declared for immediate Home Rule—"Swa Raj at once"—and thereby annulled the Moderate victory of 1909. Meanwhile, the internment in England of Mohammad Ali and Sankut Ali had made Indian Mussulmans uneasy and resentful, and this—coupled with the influence of Tilak and Mrs Besant—brought the All-India Muslim League into line with the Congress.

The capture of the Congress by the new Home Rule party, and the conversion of the Muslim League to Home Rule, commenced a new chapter in the history of Indian Nationalism.

Violence, tolerated in 1909 and 1908, was repudiated; but, with more authority and more emphasis than ever, "Swa Raj at once" was

[1] Years ago the late Mr J. H. Levy said, "Mrs Besant always speaks from some man's brief."

declared to be India's *right.* The Congress was no longer the mirror of a diversified movement, no longer a (more or less) balanced representation of various forces and opinions, it was practically a Party Caucus. It not only propounded a political programme, based upon the new ideas and worked out with much detail, but declared that programme to be binding upon every member of the Congress. This excluded the Moderates: they no longer had any organisation, they were without a voice in the Press.

Another event in 1916—outside the Congress—gave a powerful and unexpected impetus to the National Movement.

Lord Hardinge left India at a time when tension had become extreme, but men were not unhopeful, for it was understood that his Government had prepared in outline a scheme of reform. His successor was Lord Chelmsford—a Unionist peer, whose public record gave no promise of any startling departure from traditional policies. He was welcomed—if the phrase be permissible—with silent mistrust, and this mistrust was increased and made vocal by his reply to a Press deputation which waited upon him with a prayer for the repeal of the Press Act of 1911. Then the unexpected thing happened. The elected members of the Viceroy's Council—they owed their position to Lord Morley's reforms—prepared a Memorandum in which they made a strong demand for immediate reforms in the government of India. They alleged grave disabilities and galling humiliations,—they adduced (among other things) the "very sharp racial distinctions" made ("in a very offensive manner")[1] by the Arms Act, and the general disqualification of Indians for forming or joining Volunteer Corps—they asserted, with much emphasis, that it was vitally necessary to give more power to the elected representatives of the Indian people, and to modify in other ways the autocratic character of the Indian Government.

The Memorandum is very crude, and signs of hasty composition are conspicuous in it, but—these defects notwithstanding—it instantly became something very like a Declaration of Rights,—Nationalist India talked of nothing else. The main principles of this Memorandum were endorsed by the Congress, and not by the Congress alone—they were endorsed also by the Muslim League, and they became the basis of the Congress League Scheme which those two bodies (united for the first time) jointly put forth.

The events of which we have just spoken were purely Indian. Indian Nationalism has, however, ceased to be a private affair. The world is at war[2] for the rights of nationalities, the principle of national self-determination—proclaimed by the self-emancipated Russian people amidst blood

[1] These words are Dr Nair's.

[2] These words were written in the summer of 1918.

and fire—has been accepted and approved in the British Parliament by all the political leaders of the British people. Thus has Indian Nationalism become part of a world-movement. And this is not all. During this war-time Indian Nationalism has been given an international *status*, for—somewhat embarrassingly—the claims of India have been taken up into the declared intentions of German Imperialism and the Russian Revolution. Even Unionist England is beginning to think—what the Labour Party has already said—that the political and moral situation requires England to strengthen herself by recognising India's right. Outside the England that is Anglo-Indian, the insistent *Non possumus* of former days is rarely (if ever) heard.

To a large extent, this change in English public opinion is the response of a generous nature to India's notable participation in the War.

Indians who were in England during the last months of 1914 will remember the wave of enthusiasm that passed over the land when it became generally known that Indian troops were in France. In that enthusiasm there was something which made it more than a welcome to reinforcements—something which made it a welcome to *friends.* And whatever else has been impaired by this war, that " something " has not been impaired. Rather has it been much strengthened. On many a battlefield Indians and British have fought side by side and have died together for the common cause.

In the most representative Council of the Empire, India has spoken, for the first time, through native voices. In these things, and in such things, we see the birth of a new unity,—of *a new kind* of unity. The free peoples of the Empire have tacitly recognised in the peoples of India their brothers in the world's noblest peerage,—the peerage of the Empire's freedom. British and Indian statesmanship has now to make that recognition a political *act*,—so that those who speak for India, in her equal place in the Imperial Commonwealth, shall be the spokesmen of a life that is free *at home*.

CHAPTER VI

THE INDIAN STATES AND INDIAN NATIONALISM

The political problem in India is peculiarly complicated by the existence of what are called "Native States,"—that is, States which are not directly under British administration.

This fact has not yet received sufficient attention, either in England or in India. The number and variety of these Indian principalities,—diversified by wide differences in status, power, and government,—constitute a difficulty of no ordinary kind for the advocates of Swa Raj. It is not as though these Indian States could be left out of account, for a very slight consideration will show that their life is integral in India's life, their future inseparable from that of the larger Indian communities around them.

This chapter is intended:

(*a*) to show the several ways in which the Nationalist Parties have attempted to solve that problem;

(*b*) to give some idea of the relations which now subsist between the Native States and the Government of India;

(*c*) to indicate the principal changes that will

have to be made in those relations if India as a whole—*l'Inde-entière*—is to become a self-governing unit in the British Empire.

We will begin with two prime facts:

(1) The Native States include one-third of the area and one-fifth of the population of India.

Clearly, then, it is with no small thing that we have to deal, but with a much diversified population nearly as large as Germany's, and this is ruled by a proud and potent aristocracy which even the great and politic Government of India has wisely thought fit to conciliate.

(2) We speak of Native States collectively, and, if we be not careful, this convenience of speech may easily betray us into presuming a political uniformity which does not exist. Hyderabad and Madanipalli are both Native States,—the Nizam of the one and the Nawab of the other are both ruling princes. But every Indian knows how wide and important are the differences which subsist within these verbal identities. The Native States cannot be dealt with as though they were all on one footing,—least of all can they be so dealt with when we come to consider them as factors in the Home Rule Problem.

In England, the Native States are often spoken

of as "Feudatory States." The term is wholly inapplicable. The essence of the feudal relation is to be found in the vassal's homage and his fief. But the rulers of the Native States are not vassals, and their States are not fiefs. The Government of India is the paramount power, but its supremacy is not that of a feudal over-lord.

Yet it is quite clear that the Native States—even the most considerable of them—have but an imperfect sovereignty. For instance, in a famous Resolution of the Government of India,—passed on the 21st of August 1891,—it was laid down quite plainly that the principles of International Law have no bearing on the relations between the Government of India (as representing the Queen-Empress) on the one hand and the Native States under the suzerainty of Her Majesty on the other.

In every case there is a division of sovereignty between the Native State and the Government of India. How much remains with the one, and how much is exercised by the other—*that* depends, in each several case, upon a variety of facts, and ultimately upon some treaty, convention, or understanding. As Sir Henry Maine pointed out,—in a Minute which he wrote as Law Member of the Viceroy's Cabinet,—in every one of the chief cases there is some treaty or express engagement, and around each of these primary documents there has grown up a veritable maze (one might almost say "jungle") of concessions, precedents, and verbal agreements, and the actual division of sovereignty is the resultant of all these various acts.

Ever since the Crown resumed the political powers of the East India Company, and (as a consequence) came directly into relation with the Native States, there has been a marked tendency —uninterrupted, although not uniform—towards an increase of imperial power at the expense of the Native States. On the whole, the Native States have practically less independence than they had years ago. Diplomatic changes apart, there has been an imperial "penetration." A besetting power has become a pervading influence, and that pervading influence has created a common political sentiment. To-day there is in India an imperial unity which did not exist fifty years ago. Further, the political unification of India has not been merely a subjection of the Native States to the British Raj, it has been a vital integration with British India. The peoples of the Native States and those of British India have virtually become *one* people—parts of that great whole, that vast *complexus* of life and work, called *India*.

The Native States and their rulers, say the Anglo-Indian journalists—it is their stock argument—will never tolerate Nationalism. What degree of truth there is in this will become evident in the next few paragraphs. For the moment, we admit frankly that (from the Home Rule point of view) the Native States are backward,—the people have been slow to respond to the call of Nationalism, the rulers have taken most conservative views of political progress. We admit, too, that—until lately—the Nationalists themselves have not given much attention to the Native States, or taken the sentiments of their peoples and rulers into account.

The earlier Nationalists envisaged self-government as a matter which concerned only the peoples of British India. They scarcely believed—at least, it was not with them an effective conviction—that the Native States were really parts of India. In fact, the National Congress forgot—as all *bourgeois* movements are apt to forget—everything but its own immediate and particularising interests. It had not seen the prophetic vision of an India one and indivisible,—without distinction of British, Indian, French or Portuguese ; it had not recognised that wonderful unity which lies hidden beneath the diversity of Indian life and manners.

The first Congress-men left the Native States out of their programme, and watched administrative experiments in the more progressive of them with amused contempt. This had its natural result. The Native States (in their turn) left the Congress and the National Movement alone, and (in some cases) lent a not unwilling ear to those Anglo-Indian politicians who are always ready to discredit any independent effort on the part of Indians.

In the first years of its existence the National Congress either did not perceive that the Native States are an inseparable part of the political problem of India, or was guided by the tacit presupposition—totally false—that British India alone mattered. It is certain that the failure of the Congress Movement was largely due to the indifference with which its first leaders regarded the princely aristocracy of India and to the lack of a clearly defined policy with regard to the Native States.

It is only after the rapid growth of the Home Rule Party [1] into predominance that a more or less clear policy with regard to the Native States has been put forth. The effect has been instantaneous. The Native States no longer look upon themselves as separate entities,—no longer cling to the poor ambition of increasing their independence. A change has taken place in the attitude of the ruling princes which is not unlike that which modified the attitude of the English baronage after the reign of Henry II. Our princes have now definitely set aside the narrow ambitions of particularism,—the small ambition of being unconsidered rulers of negligible independent States, —and they have accepted the *rôle* of a constitutional aristocracy, an aristocracy with diminished

[1] This Party is sometimes called the Federalist Party, because it looks forward to a Federal Empire. It seems better, however, to restrict the word "Federalist" to the Movement which intends a Federal *India*—the Movement so ably championed by Dr Nair.

sovereign rights, but with an eminent part in the development of Indian polity and the guidance of Imperial policy.

The achievement of self-government by India, then, would not mean merely an "Indianising" of the legislative and administrative machinery of British India. It would mean also the development of an Indian polity in which *all* India would be equally included. The process of achievement must begin with a political transformation of British India,—and that transformation (we think) should be complete and instant,—but the rest must come gradually. Home Rule for British India should be brought about completely by some *Fiat Lux*, but a National Indian Empire—*imperium in imperio*—must come, "by slow degrees, and more and more." During the period of its gradual coming, there will be many problems to solve, many difficulties to overcome.

The first question we have to face is this: What right has the people of British India over the Native States? The suzerainty of the British Crown over the Native States is quite comprehensible. By treaties, by the right of conquest, by understandings, or in virtue of facts which were not disputed, the British Crown has established an imperial sway over the Native States. They are bound to the British Government of India as subordinate allies. But, when the Central

Government of India passes into Indian hands, will it still be able to claim—with any shadow of moral justification—such a suzerainty over the Native States? If a responsible and representative Government be established in British India, will the Native States be bound—*morally* bound—to acknowledge that Government as paramount? It is quite clear that the people of British India have *no* claim to supremacy over their brethren in the Native States. What, then, would be the normal relation between those States and the new Indian Government at Delhi?

We set aside, as impracticable and inexpedient, the policy advocated by certain extreme Nationalists who contend—misled by what happened in Italy—that the Indian principalities should be swept away. We set aside also the ultra-Conservative contention that the subsisting relations should be allowed to continue,—that the Nationalist Government at Delhi should exercise the authority now exercised by the Government of India.

The good-will of the Indian princes is essential to the success of the Nationalist—the Home Rule—movement. It is obvious, therefore, that some arrangement satisfactory to both parties—to the ruling princes and to the Nationalists of British India—must be arrived at.

The National Congress seems to have held that the existing division of India into six hundred and twenty States should be perpetuated. Those who thus think seem to have adopted the obscurantist motto, "These things *are*: let them be." Neither from the past history nor from the present character of the Native States, nor from any future that Indian patriotism can define for them, is it possible to infer any argument in favour of a division of territory and sovereignty which localises in a few square miles power sufficient to oppress and hinder, but does not provide room for efficient government. No one who has looked at the problem closely will dissent from this, or would guarantee the *status quo* to all the six hundred and twenty ruling princes of India.

The Montague-Chelmsford Report recognises that the relations which now subsist will have to be altered. It draws a broad line of demarcation between the States which have complete and independent powers of internal administration and those which have not such powers. States which fall within the first category are to be placed in direct relation with the reformed Government of India. The Report justly contends that the position of these larger States should not be in any way modified to their disadvantage. As for the States of the second category,—those minor States which are now virtually controlled by the political agents of the Government of India,—the Report seems to intend that these shall be *merged*,—their rulers being left with princely titles.

Every Nationalist will welcome these recommendations,—based (as they are) upon clear recognition of a difference which is fundamental in the problem of the Native States.

The larger Native States are really self-governing units within Britain's India Empire. Their primary relation is to the Viceroy as the local representative of the British Crown. That, however, is not their only relation. They are not separate States in a continent of States, but are members in a political unity, and their membership infers distinctive obligations. The self-governing Native States have duties, not only to the British Crown, but also to India as a whole. The Maharajah of Bikanir expressed this truth clearly when—speaking in London—he characterised the Native States as so many parts of the Indian Commonwealth,—parts united to each other and to the whole, not only by political ties, but also by natural moral obligations. This vital incorporation of the Native States in that great organism which we call "India" furnishes a complete answer to those Anglo-Indian journalists who try to hinder the movement for self-government by contending that self-government would destroy the relations which now subsist between the Native States and the Empire. The present political relation between the larger States and the Crown would continue to subsist integrally, but it would be realised in new duties,—in duties arising out of the integration of those States, with the rest of India, in the new Indian Commonwealth.

If the preservation of those larger States be a vital necessity for the steady and orderly progress of India, the gradual mediatising of the minor princes is a matter of no less importance. The argument for mediatisation is twofold. In the first place, those minor States are so small that they cannot have an independent life. They cannot be governed as they should be governed except as parts of a larger whole. It is impossible to think of them as self-contained and self-sufficient units. In their case it is quite clear that particularism would mean retrogression. In the second place, the existing division into hundreds of States entails a multiplication of governing agencies which is unnecessary and wasteful. Each of these minor Courts requires numerous ornamental and dignified institutions for which a country as poor as India can ill afford to pay. In the new India for which we are working, the mediatised princes would retain all the dignity and influence that a noble tradition and exalted fame can give, they would enjoy without restriction their ancestral possessions and personal wealth, and—set free from the cares of administration—would be able to give themselves up (without distraction) to the patriotic duties which are proper to an honoured and splendid aristocracy. *Noblesse oblige*,—that immemorial motto of their order,—points them to a pre-eminent *rôle* which is narrowed rather than enlarged by sovereignty in miniature. Becoming mediatised, they would exchange pomp without power for large opportunities for effective leadership in their common country's higher life. India as a whole is a larger sphere for patriotic service than a few square miles of Indian land.

The argument that India cannot afford to pay for the present multiplicity of administrative institutions requires more elaboration.

At the present moment there are more than six hundred States in India. A few of these are mere private estates which severally infer to the owners a certain measure of jurisdiction and certain rights of sovereignty. At least four hundred, however, are real States, with the ordinary administrative institutions of a State. Except in about fifty cases, these have no valid *ratio essendi*. Such States as Kashmir, Mysore and Travancore would certainly be autonomous members of the Indian Commonwealth. But take the case of Cochin. It is far from being the smallest of the Indian States, it is one of the best governed, it is one of the richest. Yet, in the coming Commonwealth, it could hardly claim to be autonomous. Its excellent Government-machine seems largely superfluous. Why, for example, should it have a separate Chief Court, a separate postal system, a separate military establishment? Were this administrative separateness abolished, the saving would be far from inconsiderable, and, if a similar saving were made in each of the minor States, the amount set free would be immense. To Englishmen a lac of rupees does not seem much, but if we save (on an average) a lac of rupees in each of five hundred cases, we save in all five hundred lacs, and, in India, five hundred lacs of rupees is a large sum.

It has been said that the people of the Native States do not take much interest in national politics, and are, in fact, generally indifferent to the fate of British India. To a certain extent this is true. The larger Native States enjoy self-government in all internal matters. Consequently, their people have not the grievances which are a chief source of Nationalism in British India. "The economic drain," the legal exploitation, the practical monopoly of the higher offices by men who are really foreigners, the many humiliations consequent upon political inferiority,—these things, omnipresent and keenly felt in British India, do not touch the self-governing States. Nevertheless, the people of those States—moved by kinship and by community in patriotism—give an undivided support to the Nationalists of British India in their demand for Home Rule. They recognise that the present state of affairs restricts their own outlook and narrows their own sphere of action, and they see that this de-vitalising fact cannot be done away with except in a self-governing Indian Commonwealth. They have discovered that their own weal and woe are not separate and private things, but are bound up for ever with the weal and woe of their kinsmen in the rest of India.

This new feeling of solidarity is not merely popular,—it is shared by the ruling princes. In unmistakable terms the Maharajah of Bikanir and the Maharajah of Baroda have both given expression to it. This consciousness of *unity*—it is an increasing consciousness—is a fact of the very first importance for the future of the Indian Motherland.

The discovery of India's vital and moral unity has removed one of the last obstacles to the achievement of self-government. *It makes India a nation*, and opens up the way for it to take a nation's place—a *free* nation's place—in the British Commonwealth of States.

By awakening into their unity, the peoples of India have created a new situation. Every one sees it, and sees that it is new: the presence of the Maharajah of Bikanir and Sir S. P. Sinha at the first Imperial War Conference, as representatives of India, is evidence—almost proof—that Great Britain and the Dominions accept it.

CHAPTER VII

INDIA AND THE EMPIRE

It must be confessed that for Indians the word "Empire" has always had repellent associations. It has seemed to them a synonym for racial superiority and "economic exploitation." They have identified "the imperial idea" with the doctrine that "Trade follows the Flag"—a doctrine which they have heard described as the golden chain that binds India to England—and this had led them to surmise that imperialism is another name for aggressive commercialism. This dislike of imperialism has been increased by the racial pride of the Hindus. That pride resents the covert assertion of inferiority in "the White Man's Burden"; it resents more bitterly the hostile attitude—felt as an insult—of the Dominions.

The truth should be told quite plainly. The Dominions, which seem to be pillars of the Empire, well-nigh made an Indian imperialism impossible. At this moment, Australia excludes Indians by a strict and fantastic enforcement of an arbitrary language test. Canada, which does not exclude either Chinese or Japanese, has put up a very effective barrier against Indians in the shape of "the continuous voyage law." That law prohibits the landing of all Indians who have not made a "continuous voyage" from their native land. As there is no direct mercantile or passenger service between India and Canada, the prohibition amounts to a general exclusion. Before the passing of the Act, some five thousand Indians went to Canada, but they were not allowed to take their wives with them.

Above all, however, it was the treatment of Indians in the Transvaal and Natal—and, indeed, in every part of South Africa—that made imperialism odious to educated Indians, and the Empire suspect. Indian labour has been a considerable factor in the development of the Transvaal, and even to-day the prosperity of that country depends (to no small extent) upon the large resident Indian community. Yet the treatment of Indians in the Transvaal has made Anglo-Indians and Nationalists unanimous in protest.

It will be remembered that the treatment of Indians by the Boers was one of the reasons advanced for the South African War. No doubt the Boer Government treated Indians badly. That Government, however, was amenable to pressure from Downing Street as no Colonial Government is. After the Transvaal became incorporated into the Empire, the position of the Transvaal Indians became worse. Their children—born in wedlock, the offspring of marriages solemnised according to ancestral rites—were declared to be illegitimate;

a poll-tax of £3 was levied upon them; they were not allowed to hold real estate or to own mining rights; they were excluded from trams and from the first- and second-class carriages on railways. Indignities in Africa raised a tempest in India, and the tempest invaded imperial policy when Lord Hardinge, the Viceroy,—rightly interpreting a general mood,—declared plainly that the Government of India would stand by its people abroad.

The Indians in South Africa—*British* South Africa—did not take this "lying down." They found an energetic leader in M. K. Ghandi, and had recourse to those characteristically modern weapons—passive resistance and a political strike. Then the imperial authorities intervened—*against the Indians.* This misdirected intervention had large consequences in India. Even the Moderates were shaken—the Moderates, who had pinned their faith to the British Flag, and had been proud to proclaim themselves citizens of the British Empire. What did they see when they looked across the Ocean to South Africa? Indians insulted, degraded, oppressed: the Empire unable or unwilling to protect them.

By these events, the Indians of India were awakened to the real position of India within the Empire, and the awakening was a rude one. It is not surprising that, when it was proposed to establish closer relations between India and the Dominions, Indians of all parties and all shades of opinion united in opposition. "The Imperial connection" was universally discredited.

This unpopularity of the imperial principle has been the chief hindrance to the acceptance by Indians of that federal re-constitution of the Empire which is the necessary corollary of Swa Raj. Distrust of the Dominions was so deep-rooted in India that there would have been irreconcilable opposition to any scheme which proposed to set up a central imperial authority to control imperial affairs. As India is the pivot on which the defence of the Empire turns, a central authority charged with the defence of the Empire would almost be bound to interfere in Indian affairs. Were the defence of the Empire to remain in the hands of the British Cabinet—which is supposed to stand above the narrow gospel of "Whitemanity" which the Dominions preach—Indian Home Rulers would have been content (provided India were given Home Rule for all internal affairs) to see in the Secretary of State for India the representative of India in all matters relating to defence. But they did not take kindly to the idea of a central imperial authority composed chiefly of British and Colonial politicians. They feared—and South Africa made their fear reasonable—that such a Council would be dominated by the doctrine of "white supremacy," by the prejudice of the "colour-line," and would be predisposed to regard Indians as helots.

That is one part of the story. Now for the other.

Indians who had given close attention to the politics of Middle and Eastern Asia recognised two things quite clearly. They recognised :

(1) that India is the most vulnerable part of the Empire ;

(2) that all liberties and national claims within the Empire must be, and ought to be, subordinate to the security of the general Commonwealth, *i.e.* of the Empire as a whole.

This recognition made a change in their outlook. It gave them a point of view from which Indian affairs—*e.g.* defence and relations with foreign States—were seen as *Commonwealth affairs.* The advent of Japan as a Great Power, the approach of Germany to the Persian Gulf through her alliance with Turkey, and to the borders of Afghanistan through the disruption of the Tzarish Empire—these things became factors in the problem of Indian Home Rule, for they made it clear to Indian minds that the political progress of India is conditioned by the general safety of the Empire. Thus " the Imperial connection " took a new form in the thoughts of Indian Nationalism—it became the safeguard of a political idea. Men saw that, ultimately, the interests of India and the interests of the Empire are identical, and this perception of identity became an *act* when Mr Shaji moved, in the Legislative Council, that the Imperial Conference should include representatives of India. As we all know, the Government of India accepted Mr Shaji's motion and commended it to London. The commendation was effectual, and—upon the invitation of the Imperial Government—native representatives of India sat on the Imperial Conference of 1917. Every one saw that India's public *status* within the Empire had undergone a change. That invitation by the Imperial Government created new relations, not only between India and Great Britain, but also between India and the Dominions.

At that conference of 1917 Sir S. P. Sinha was one of the representatives of India and Ian Smuts one of the representatives of South Africa. The former had been president of the National Congress, the latter had made himself notorious during the protective strike of the Indians in South Africa. The very fact that these two men sat together, in conference on the future of the Empire, showed how great a change the war had brought about in the British Empire,—the Empire was becoming its true self in an actual Commonwealth. The same fact—the co-operation of two men so different—showed also the true line of development for Indian Nationalism, a line which until then had been obscured by the prejudice of "the colour-line" on the one hand, and by resentment of much injustice on the other.

The deliberations of the Imperial Conference of 1917 led to an equitable settlement based upon statutory equality and consequent reciprocity. This settlement was elaborated and developed by the Imperial War Cabinet and the Conference of 1918, and thus the last obstacle—the last *Indian* obstacle—to a closer integration of the Empire was removed.

The relations between India and the Dominions will be based, in future, upon the principle of reciprocity. If Indians in Canada be excluded from the franchise, the Government of India will have a recognised right to deprive Canadians in India of their votes for the Legislative Council. If it be enacted in British Columbia that no Hindu firm may employ Canadian girls as typewriters, the Government of India will have a recognised right to say that Columbians in India may not have Indian cooks. If South Africans persist in excluding Indians from trams and first-class railway carriages, South Africans in India will become liable to a similar exclusion. The acceptance of this principle—the principle of reciprocity—by the Dominions assures to Indians equality of right in every Dominion. That assurance strikes at the root of India's well-founded mistrust—a mistrust which has hitherto inhibited the growth of an Indian imperial sentiment.[1]

We now approach the end of an argument. The British Empire is *consociatio consociationum* ;

[1] To the Englishman who has helped in the writing of this book the settlement indicated does not seem either practical or final.

its normal unity subsists in a common sentiment. Can that sentiment become a common sentiment in India? We know what the Empire means to those who live in and by the great English tradition[1]—can it be made to mean the same to Indians? We who write these pages—an Indian and an Englishman—believe that it can be. If aberrant policies which disguise selfishness disappoint our hope, the disappointment will show that England's tradition is no longer England's life. British imperialism will be little more than political commercialism if, unto the 325 millions of India, it be not the assurance of *freedom*—of free citizenship in a free Commonwealth of free States.[2]

To most Englishmen, events in Asia seem remote things,—of obscure significance and of only indirect interest. Yet the political re-birth of

[1] See Appendices IV. and V.

[2] This fact has been prominently set forth in England by an earnest band of workers, of whom Mr Lionel Curtis is the best known. Mr Curtis—after publishing those noteworthy books, *The Problem of the Commonwealth* and *The Commonwealth of Nations*—addressed himself to the imperial aspect of the Indian problem. He brought to his new studies an academical equipment not often excelled, a judgment prepared by earlier study of similar problems elsewhere and by practical experience gained by administrative work in South Africa. The result of his latest studies has been given to the world in a volume entitled *Letters to the People of India on Responsible Government*. He arrives at the conclusion that the development of representative and responsible government is the most urgent of the problems that immediately confront British statesmanship in India, and must be taken in hand before the ultimate solution of the

Asia is one of the salient facts of the twentieth century, and it has become the main factor in what may be called the *external* problem of Indian self-government. In modern times, the shifting vortex of international politics has never been as near India as it is to-day.

Whatever international re-settlement be resultant from this war, it will not be final. England will not be able to maintain her position in the world—will not be able to follow the vocation her noblest sons discern for her in the East—without the co-operation of India. That co-operation can be had, but it must be—*co-operation in freedom.*

A great opportunity has come to the English people. If they be equal to it, they will make the Empire which is their glory the greatest fraternity the world has ever seen. If they be equal to it, they will knit India to England and England to India in a free partnership that will never be broken. But only in one way can that opportunity be used as it should be used—*the*

purely imperial problem can be approached. That ultimate solution he finds in a federal union between the various members of the British Commonwealth—including a self-governing India. He recognises the difficulty created by the general interest of the Empire in the defence of India, and he proposes to meet that difficulty by placing the North-Western Frontier Province outside the authority of the New Indian Government. He would have that Province directly administered by the new Imperial Cabinet. This would give India as much voice as any other part of the Empire in the defence of what would then be a common frontier—Imperial rather than Indian—and would leave her internal autonomy unrestricted.

freedom that has been the strength of England must be made the strength of India also.

By many and divers names has Freedom variously interpreted herself to men: the name she has chosen for herself in India—what is it? *Swa Raj!*[1]

[1] It should not be forgotten that Swa Raj means much more than control of the parish pump. It means *political power*,—the right to opportunity in its complete political form. (For the right to opportunity, see *National Revival*.)

SUPPLEMENTARY CHAPTER

Received from the Burma Deputation

NATIONALISM IN BURMA

BURMA is at present, politically, part of the British Indian Empire, with an area of over 230,000 square miles and a population of over twelve millions. Her people had an ancient civilisation of their own, and on more than one occasion made their influence felt over the major portion of the Indo-Chinese peninsula. They, for the most part, profess Buddhism—non-Buddhists being but a small minority. They are practically homogeneous, and the Burmese language is spoken all over the country. The Burmese are a democratic and freedom-loving race, and their women enjoy a freer and higher position than women in any Asiatic country. Burma has by far the highest standard of literacy in the Indian Empire, and has been wholly untouched by seditious movements. Caste distinction, class hatred, or sectarian rancour find no place in the Burmese national character.

With the Burmese the sentiment of nationality has always been a living thing. This feeling permeates and dominates their history as the Irrawaddy dominates the land in which they dwell, and, like that river, it broadens in its course. Nor is the reason far to seek. The Burmese inhabit a country girt about and isolated by broad barriers of almost pathless mountains. On the west, except for the small stretch of the Kaladan, the Chin and Naga Hills rear a nearly impassable bulwark against incursions from India. Northward lies the rugged mountains of the Chinese frontier, whence, on the Eastern borders, the Shan States plateau and fold upon fold of mountains shut off Burma from Siam. On the south and south-west the coasts are washed by the Bay of Bengal. At the present day it is practically all one people which dwells within this iron ring of mountains. Both the Talaings and Karens in Lower Burma, though linguistically separate, are ethnically close akin to the Burmese. The former are fast being absorbed into them, and though foreign missionary influences have so far prevented a section of the Karens from sharing that fate, the probabilities are that, sooner or later, it will overtake them. Always the dominating and more civilised nation absorbs the scattered tribes. Moreover, from the conquest of the Talaings by the Burmese (A.D. 1755) until the advent of the British, the country was ruled by the Burmese kings sufficiently long to establish a strong national tradition. This tradition, combined with the common Buddhist religion, common customs, and a common social framework, has developed a strong feeling of nationality. Man has completed what

Nature began. Here in this giant horse-shoe of mountains Nature said: "Behold my cradle for a nation!" The Burmese are that predestined nation.

The loss of Lower Burma—Tennaserim and Arakan in 1825 and Pegu in 1852—was for the Burmese kings a rankling sore. They ever cherished the hopes of its recovery. (Does not the great statue still stand on Mandalay Hill, pointing in remembrance ever to the South?) But instead, Upper Burma itself fell in 1886. After King Theebaw's surrender, large bands of Burmese soldiers took up arms and opposed the British occupation of Upper Burma. But owing to the superiority of the British army these bands became weakened and broken up. Their *morale* also degenerated, and they committed a thousand outrages. For eight years or more both provinces became the scene of violent disturbances. This armed opposition sprang from the feelings of patriotism, and the bands were at first composed of patriots as keen as Hereward the Wake. They hoped against hope to expel the English, to restore their king. Though veiled in the face of irresistible force, the grief of the people was real. "You have made us like Kalas (Indians)," said a typical Burman. "We are no longer a people; we no longer have a king to reign over us." Under the firm, if narrow, administration of the British, peace has long prevailed; trade and commerce have multiplied; railways, roads and steamers provide easy communications; many a thousand acres, once sterile jungle, are now furrowed by the ploughs. In material prosperity Burma has advanced by leaps and bounds. But the material condition of the people have become worse—for they are poorer; and always has lived the feeling of nationality; always pride of race and the thought of the good old days and the bygone kings.

Difference of race and language, and the long leagues of sea, at first hindered Burma from joining the modern national movement in India. But ideas know no frontier. Though governments frown on them, and censors fain would bar them out, the winds whisper them, the clouds carry them along, the sunlight blazons them abroad. The movement in Burma towards self-government began in 1906. Expanding slowly at first, it broke out into sudden vigour with the declaration of 20th August 1917. This quick development took the officials by surprise, just as the outbreaks after the annexation of Upper Burma took them by surprise. Bureaucracy loves to see in the peoples it rules only docile children,—patriotism is a sentiment reserved for Englishmen. At the most, a subject people may cultivate the Imperial Idea, of which there was a fatuous official cult in Burma. When coloured people show patriotism, this "aristocracy of skin" denies, scoffs, denounces. So it has been in India and so in Burma. Did not the Lieutenant-Governor, Sir R. Craddock, a typical official, at first deny the existence of the national movement? Later on (December 1918), he was constrained reluctantly to admit it. As in Canada, Ireland, Egypt, India—in fact, in every part of the Empire, except Australasia, which has claimed the right of self-government for which Britain, in theory at least, fought the war—the governing class has ranted loudly of "agitators"—"Young Burma"—are the young the only patriots?—"loyalty of the respectable classes"—and so forth. The individuals change, but the jargon does not change. In one respect only has officialdom blessed the movement. There has been no "sedition" or "anarchy," and this by the admission of Sir R. Craddock himself, he who, at the passing of the Rowlatt Act, saw all India seething in "anarchy." As a matter of fact, "anarchy" is merely the name which enemies of the nationalist movement in India give to sedition, just as the Austrians and their friends dubbed "anarchists" the wilder spirits in the Italian *Risorgimento*. If you repress public meetings, muzzle the Press, issue *lettres de cachet* against popular leaders, and fetter generally the liberties of the people, you are looking for sedition, and you will assuredly find it. The movement in Burma, coming relatively late in the day, will attain its goal before blundering officialdom have had time or opportunity to goad young hot-bloods to fury. Not that officialdom has favoured it one whit more than in India—simply time has been lacking to produce untoward results.

On his memorable visit to India in 1917-18 Mr Montagu could not find time to visit Burma. Though he received deputations from that Province in Calcutta, their representations naturally did not affect him as much as if he had toured the country. Hence he was induced by those, whose real object was to keep Burma apart from the flowing tide of Indian democracy, to direct that Burma should be treated separately from the Indian Provinces. The grounds given were that the people were different and their problems altogether different. In reality the Burmese do not differ from the Indians more than some races of Indians differ from each other. Pali, an Indian language, holds in their speech precisely the same position as Latin in English, the Buddhist religion is of Indian origin, and the Government of India, in its laws and regulations, has never made any distinction between Burma and the other Provinces. Moreover, it is not here a question of *problems*, but of the *machinery* for dealing with problems.

Sir R. Craddock, after in vain trying to foist on the Burmese an Advisory Council, finally, after great delay, put forward a Scheme in which, to quote from the Indian *Moral and Material Progress Report*, "diarchy" and Parliamentary responsibility—the two leading principles of the Montagu-Chelmsford proposals—found no place." Its cardinal features were indirect elections in the rural areas, with electoral colleges consisting mainly of village headmen, *i.e.* of officials, a big-area grouping of the towns, and irresponsible Ministers —one a non-official European—nominated by the Lieutenant-Governor and removable at his pleasure. In a word, a puppet Assembly and puppet Ministers. There was no control over the Budget.

A storm of opposition swept the country. The Burmese perceived that although in many ways —by absence of caste, language difficulties, and religious feuds, by their democratic society and their superior primary education—more suited than India for an advanced scheme of self-government, Sir R. Craddock's proposals would place them in a kind of political backwater, on a level with the Frontier Province and "backward tracts." Patriotism, self-respect, an earnest desire for progress, combined to add wings to an agitation which soon embraced practically the whole of Burma. The Young Men's Buddhist Association, a society founded in 1906, partly for philanthropic and partly for political purposes, took the lead, and other societies—some of them established many years before the Young Men's Buddhist Association—followed suit. Quite a number of new societies, working to the same end, have sprung up since the announcement of 20th August 1917 was made. These national societies, numbering over 220 branches spread all over the country, have amalgamated themselves, and have been actively at work under the management of a general council appointed by themselves. The national Press—both vernacular and Anglo-vernacular—ranged itself on the popular side. The primary object of the agitation was to obtain for Burma the reforms given to the major provinces of the Indian Empire—surely a very moderate request. Meetings were held, speeches delivered, and an active propaganda set on foot in towns and villages. Patriotism, love of country, so long repressed, welled up anew. None urged separation from the Empire, but all desired, and passionately desired, a self-governing Burma, a nation amongst the nations. The Baptist Karens, under missionary influence, held somewhat aloof from the movement. On the other hand, Indians and Chinese, with a true patriotism, made common cause with the Burmese. As in India, the opposition consisted almost solely of official and non-official Europeans, a class insignificant in numbers but possessing great political influence. Love of place and power led on the former, whilst the latter hoped to retain a profitable monopoly of trade, a tradition of the days of John Company. To both the feeling of patriotism that moves all Asia is a sealed book. Patriotism is, in their eyes, a virtue solely for white men, or, rather, for Britain and her allies. Elsewhere it is an offence. They think exactly as the Canadian British thought in the first half of the seventeenth century, or as Ulstermen think to-day. Not for the first time privilege and race ascendancy face democracy, freedom and equal rights. The end is not doubtful, and the end is near.

A deputation representative of the reform movement, consisting of Maung Pu, Maung Ba Pe and Maung Tun Shein, left in July 1919 to present the case for Burma to the Joint Committee on the Government of India Bill. Maung Pu gave his evidence before that Committee on 19th August. The Committee, in their Report, did not recommend the inclusion of Burma, but they stated (paragraph 8) that, "The Burmese have deserved and should receive a constitution analogous to that provided by the Bill for their Indian fellow-subjects." On 28th November the Deputation and Mr Houghton had an interview with Mr Montagu, and received from him a satisfactory assurance as to the future constitution of Burma. Repeating this assurance on 3rd December in the House of Commons, he said, "What Burma is anxious for is to come to Parliament itself, and not to be left to the tender mercies either of the Secretary of State, the Government of India, or the local Government. I quite agree with the Joint Committee. Burma is not India, but Burma must get an analogous grant of self-government, a similar grant of self-government, subject to differences in the local conditions of Burma. . . . The real case, therefore, is that Burma will get without loss of time one of two things. It will either become a Governor's Province—if that turns out to be the best solution—and in that case it will be dealt with under Clause 15: if, however, it wishes to have a different Constitution, say, from the rest of India, then we shall have to have new legislation, which will be introduced without loss of time into Parliament." When further pressed by Mr G. R. Thorne, Colonel Wedgwood and others to state the time when a Bill for Burma would be introduced, Mr Montagu said, "It is obvious that I cannot give a definite promise to-night that I will introduce legislation next Session, because I am not the custodian of our Parliamentary time. I do not know who may be Secretary of State for India next year, and I have not a freehold of my position. I hope and desire not to leave this work undone, and I want to bring in a Bill next year. I am now in telegraphic communication with the Government of India upon the Burmese scheme, and I shall be very much surprised if at the end of next Session we have not passed the Bill dealing with Burma."

Burma, therefore, now stands at the threshold of representative government. The hands that would fain detain her in the old discredited tutelage have been set aside. Soon she will be free to advance, like the other Provinces of the Indian Empire, towards the full development of her national genius, her national culture and her national aspirations. In no part of that Empire will the progress towards self-government be more interesting; in no part does it hold out higher hopes, both material and moral. Material, because Burma, already rich, has greater undeveloped natural wealth than any other Province; moral, because, under the influence of the Buddhist religion, we may expect great things in education, in the control of liquor and drugs, and in the elevation of the people to a democracy of high ideals.

APPENDIX I

The Englishman who has helped in the writing of this book has received a letter which he may not disregard,—because of a friendship informed (from his side) by much respect.

The letter was a comment upon another attempt to commend Indian Nationalism to the British peoples. This is what it said:

> "3. The author does not touch on the root-difficulty of the thinking Englishman. Liberty, Home Rule, popular government, or whatever it is called, is an entire stranger to the East. Indeed, it is solely an English discovery, and no nation, beginning with France, has adopted it without a period of bloodshed and reaction. If this is the case next door to England, how can we abandon lightly the 'strong hand' which is the traditional method of Eastern politics, and which, wielded by English justice, has given India prosperity and peace such as she has never known in her long and famous history? The lamentable failure of the Turkish Committee of 'Order and Progress' and the Russian *débâcle* are not encouraging to those who *do* believe in training all races to look after themselves."

(*a*) The man who received that letter has said high things about England's history and tradition. No one is farther than he from being a minimiser in patriotism. But his passion for England's distinctive freedom—now little more than a thing scarcely remembered—does not limit his faith in freedom. What has been done here can be done elsewhere—not immediately, but (as here) gradually.

(*b*) "Gradually"—that seems to be the critical word, and yet it is not, because all (or nearly all) accept it. A people quite unversed in freedom's ways *could not* step at once into that large and temperate freedom—now obscured and disregarded—which is the chief greatness of England.

Training of some kind there must be, but by whom? It seems practically certain that no superintending bureaucracy will ever train men for freedom. Freedom herself is the sole teacher: only by exercise in freedom can a people be trained for freedom.

(*c*) The Young Turks, Paris in 1793, Petrograd in 1918—three disasters, men say. Yes, three disasters. But what brought about those disasters? Not freedom, but—in each case—the withholding of freedom by a "strong hand."

APPENDIX II

Concerning Nationality

A Supplement (written in April 1918) to an Appendix in Mr Hakluyt Egerton's *Patriotism*.

We all know that there is a Jewish race—is there also such a thing as Jewish nationality?

Were this question one that could be answered only and finally by Jewish testimony to Jewish experience, I would have no right to say anything, for I am not a Jew. But no answer to the question can be merely an adducing of experience. Before experience can become testimony in this matter we must know what nationality means. In that pre-requisite, one who is not a Jew may find permission to speak.

I

"Is there such a thing as Jewish nationality?" To me that question seems very like "Can English Jews be patriots?" Of course they can be. The answer is obvious, and admits of no debate: if we understand it thoroughly we shall understand nationality.

In the first place then—What is Patriotism? Some years ago,—in my first book,[1]—I answered that question as well as I could, and when I revise my answer to-day—in the light of the failures and achievements of this immensely tragic time—it still seems to me substantially sound. I cannot give another answer, but this war-time—which has confirmed my thoughts through much disappointment—has provided for my answer other words.

Somewhere about the time when I was writing *Patriotism*, Kipling wrote his immortal record of Faith's victory over the obvious:

> "If England was what England seems,
> And not the England of our dreams,
> But only putty, brass an' paint,
> 'Ow quick we'd chuck 'er. *But she ain't.*"

To-day "The England of our dreams" is the England of our love; at this moment we are worshipping her epiphany in those shattered ranks in France.[2]

Let every man speak for himself.

The England of my love—What is it? It is the Godward aspect of my country's life—a splendour above evident selfishness, a music beyond near discord, a greatness which narrow policies cannot impair. "The England of my love." It is a land which no geography has charted—an unseen Motherland, where the best harvest of the past is made perpetual (in super-substantial bread) for the Present's life. Here, in these English lands, uncounted generations have lived and worked and died. They have not sunk into oblivion, or passed out into a scopeless void. The worthiness they *were*, the worthiness wrought out

[1] *Patriotism: An Essay towards a Constructive Theory of Politics.* By Hakluyt Egerton.

[2] Written on Easter Day, 1918.

in them and by them—purged by Time from the stains of Time—has become immortal in a great tradition. That tradition is no remote and idle thing. It is a presence in our institutions, a predisposition in thought, an information of the heart, a silent power in the hidden foundations of character—though we discern not our sonship, we are all born of it. We are all born of it, and therefore is the England of our love our Motherland.

A fantasy? No—it is the greatness of England provided for the needs of England, and into that greatness pass all who die for England.

Patriotism is love of country,—of one's visible country. Not, however, in its apparent—its obvious—reality, is one's visible country the *source* of Patriotism, and though ever the *term* of Patriotism, not for its own sake is it the term. It is term and source *because* and as the mediation of an unseen Motherhood not less local.

Our country's name is often used as though the *mere name* were a magic charm. Men who know not the meaning of "England" send that word clamorously to others as ignorant—and expect miracles. Of course they are disappointed. But those whom England has taught can use her name effectually, because, on *their* lips, her name is her power, and because they know her unobserved preparation in the hearts of men.

That is the point—a preparation in the heart. Patriotism is not an innate virtue, nor is it unconditioned. Before it can exist, something must happen. Patriotism is love of country. Love of country there *cannot* be, unless, *in experience*, one's country has become *lovable*.

Love is the soul's response to a gift of Life. Man's natural responsiveness to vital values becomes Patriotism—when? When a Nation's common life is recognised as a *bearer of values*.

II

What has all this to do with nationality? It has much to do with nationality, because Patriotism is the chief normal correlate of national consciousness—not always, but whenever a nation's common life is a *felt value.*

By "national consciousness" I do not mean that fantastic unreality,—the consciousness of some falsely-supposed corporate personality. I mean the kind of consciousness distinctively produced in the individual by membership in a nation.

This brings us to the cardinal question: What is a Nation?

A Nation is a Society particularised by *a distinctive common consciousness* which—in its political aspect—envisages political self-determination.

A volume could be written upon this definition, but—happily—the comments required by the purpose of this paper need not extend beyond a few brief notes.

(*A*) Political self-determination makes a nation master in its own house. Therefore, political self-determination implies political sovereignty. Nevertheless, political sovereignty is not the thing that constitutes a nation.

(1) There was an effective political sovereignty in the Golden Horde. But the Golden Horde was not a Nation.

Again, one sovereignty is common to all the peoples subject to the Hungarian Crown. That common sovereignty, however, has not made Hungarians, Croats, Slovenes and Austro-Serbs *one* Nation.

(2) Some Nations are not Sovereign States.

We are beginning to speak of our Dominions over the seas as *Nations.* But not one of them is a Sovereign State.

In the first place, "the King in Parliament" can still legislate for any or all of them. In the second place, important powers of the Crown—powers which, when active, involve the Dominions[1]—are exercised only through the London Cabinet.

(3) Political sovereignty is not one of the marks of a Nation.

(*a*) In the old days of "Absolutist" Government on the Danube, the several nations under Hapsburg rule were really nations, although not one of them had political sovereignty.

Again, before Germany's deceptive establishment of a Kingdom of Poland, we rightly spoke of "the Polish Nation."

(*b*) To designate a people which is undeniably *national*, but has not any kind or degree of political sovereignty, we often use the word "nationality" instead of the word "nation."

Nationality, however, is either the quality which makes a people a nation, or the quality distinctively resultant from membership in a nation. In either case, apart from a nation there cannot be nationality.

Therefore, if there be—as there undoubtedly is—a Polish nationality wider than the now Kingdom of Poland, there is also a co-extensive Polish nation.

(To provide for the case of a nation which is entirely without political sovereignty, the definition uses the word "envisage." The constitutive common life of such a nation *looks towards* political self-determination—is, one may say, intrinsically determined to it.)

(*B*) Self-determination does not suffice to make a body politic a nation.

The Hanseatic League was a self-determining body politic. But it was not a nation.

[1] I am thinking of the powers appropriate to foreign affairs.

The crown of the German Cæsars was an imperial crown—not subject to any temporal authority or power. Therefore the Holy Roman Empire was a self-determining body politic. But this did not make the several members of that Empire *one* nation.

(*C*) A nation's political self-determination is a function of its constitutive common life.

A nation *is* a nation in virtue of a distinctive common life of a certain kind—(*vide* the definition).

III

What is the nature, and what the origin, of a nation's common life?

These questions can be answered in two words: "Comradeship" and "Co-operation."

I reproduce a few words which will never be out of date,—at least, not in any time within the scope of to-day's policies.

> "What is it that makes us English folk truly one people? Not the bare fact that, for a thousand years and more, we have lived together between the Cheviots and the Channel, but because, between the Cheviots and the Channel, we have found a common work, and wrought out a common life,—because the wasteful discipline of war and fruitful co-operation in peace, long fellowship in suffering and endeavour, and comradeship in many a fight for freedom, have overcome the differences which at first armed Northumbria against Mercia and Wessex against West Wales, Saxon against Dane, and both against Norman, and those also which later on (within the one polity of the mediæval kingdom) made the countryside half servile, the Church half-alien, and the baronage an armed oppression. It is because of these past victories of developing brotherliness over the

particularism of class and province,—and not merely because our forefathers were neighbours,—that we who to-day live upon English ground are all fellow-citizens in one free Commonwealth, partners in a common industry, inheritors of a common tradition, sharers of a common hope. We are a nation because, in some sufficing measure, we have grown together into unity of life; because, within our borders, hostility has given place to brotherhood—as yet indeed far from perfect, but even now effectively real; because the mutual helpfulness of man to man has made this English land of ours truly our home; and because, within that home, we, as members of one family, have become knit together by common purposes and by common hopes, by common sanctities and by common ideals."[1]

"Members of one family"—*that* is the point. In other words—Comradeship and Co-operation.

When a common historical experience creates a common life and a common consciousness becomes political, *a nation is born.*

IV

It will be noticed that I have said nothing about race.

Well, the Germans have said much about race, and in England—where Thought is rarer than Christianity, and equally a disqualification—national feeling is confounded with racial feeling, and the call of the Motherland is deemed "the call of the blood."[2]

Yet—the race is one thing, and the nation another. They cannot be confounded without depraving political thought, and predisposing to extensive perversions of policy.

[1] See *National Revival.*

[2] Mr Rudyard Kipling, who gives to crude thought the splendour of Art, has done much to confirm men in this mistake.

No one has ever said that race is nationality, and no one with any intrinsic claim to consideration has ever said that racial unity is indispensable to a nation. The Germans have carried the racial conception of nationality as far as anyone, and, naturally enough—since they believe this war to be, on their side, a war for Germanism—that conception is prominent in their war-time pamphlets. If, however, we look carefully at the better of those pamphlets—I know nothing of the others—we shall find that the dialectical centre is not really in the much-vaunted *race*, but in a character and life supposed to be characteristic of that race. The thing propounded is ethnological: the thing *valued* is a fact of another order—not ethnological, but psychological.

It cannot be said that race is unimportant, for a common race implies a common tradition, and points back to centuries of neighbourliness. Community of race fosters the growth of a common consciousness. Therefore it plays an important part in the gradual forming of nations. Its importance, however, is that of a *condition*, not of a *factor*, for nationality does not subsist in facts of ethnology —it subsists only in a consciousness which these, if present, help to create.[1]

A condition not a factor—to give *race* a higher standing in this matter is merely the mistake of a healthy instinct that needs enlightenment, or a prejudice of professors without political understanding.[2]

[1] (1) This finally refutes the argument which would set aside the present consciousness of annexed Alsace-Lorraine by pretended demonstrations that the people of those "lost provinces" are of German origin.

(2) In the seventeenth century, that famous Belgian, Justus Lipsius, wrote: "We Belgians are Germans." Very few Belgians would have written or said that in July 1914.

Nationality is "a content of consciousness," not a fact of ethnology.

[2] The higher kind of political understanding is the rarest thing in the world. It is even rarer than energetic friendship.

V

Whatever be the distinctions that a subtle disputant could draw, there can be no doubt that "Germanism" does, in effect, make *race* a factor—a chief factor—in the conception of nationality. Consequently, to non-Germanic subjects of the German Empire, it can offer only a choice between these two alternatives—fusion and subordination.[1]

"Fusion"—the word, appropriate enough to things physical, is out of place when used of the spiritual processes whereby men become "very members incorporate" in a national organism. For it *is* a spiritual process—this penetration (this information) of the individual by a common consciousness, this adoption into a national tradition, and it is possible only because nationality is itself spiritual—not ethnological, but psychological.

Because nationality and the process of real nationalisation are wholly spiritual, men of different races can stand together, on an equal footing, within the unity of one nationality.

At this very moment, Tamils and Sinhalese are discovering themselves to be co-ordinates in an emergent Ceylonese nation, and something of the same kind seems coming to pass in India.

What of the Jews? They also are human, and the process which I have designated "the process of real nationalisation" depends upon facts which the very constitution of human nature makes universal facts. Of course a Jew can become a good citizen in the land of his domicile—and remain a good Jew. The Jew, no less than other men, can find his nationality where he lives.

Here is the summing up of the whole matter:

Nationality subsists in a common consciousness created by comradeship and co-operation. The Jew

[1] This observation does not touch, or scarcely touches, Naumann's *Mittel-Europa*, the most statesmanlike book produced by the war.

is not incapable of comradeship, he is not incapable of co-operation, his nature is not impenetrable by a besetting common life. . . .

It were absurd to continue. Of course, a Jew can receive a nation's common consciousness, and, along with it, the nationality it infers.

Real nationalisation depends upon two things—opportunity and willingness. If any dwellers (alien or native) within the borders of a nation be debarred from comradeship and co-operation, they *cannot* be national. If any alien residents withhold themselves from comradeship, and co-operate (if at all) without real fellowship, *they* cannot be national,—*and they should not be naturalised.*[1]

APPENDIX III

The Fourth Report (1914) of the Royal Commission on the Civil, Legal, Consular and Diplomatic Services

Extract from the "Reservation" by Mr Arthur Boutwood.

Administrative Work and Education.

8. The work of the Administrative Grade in the Civil Service is a form of political government. Consequently it cannot be performed without high qualities of mind and character. An insight which can thoroughly analyse complex movements in social life, a sympathetic understanding of contemporary tendencies and of the needs and aspirations of men, knowledge that can place facts in their true relation, sound judgment, initiative, tact,

[1] Germany has furnished us, over-abundantly, with strong reasons for refusing to naturalise any Germans in future—until the advent of that far-distant day when Germany will change her heart radically.

courtesy, manliness that can assume and bear responsibility, these are characteristics of the first-class administrator, these are some of the qualities necessary for the higher work of the Civil Service.

An attempt is made to obtain these qualities by means of the Class I. Examination. That attempt is interesting, and it has apparently reached a considerable degree of success, but the evidence before the Commission does not enable one to gauge the success. This, however, seems clear—whatever be the success of the examination, that success is largely a concomitant result.

9. Men often speak with deserved disrespect of things that are proffered in the name of Education, but no one who has known the reality of Education can slight it. By it the great achievements of Art and thought and the yet greater achievements of patriotism and faith are made a present possession; by it man's environment is transfigured and his outlook indefinitely extended; without it patriotism is well-nigh blind and faith scarcely articulate. Nor are the results of Education merely intellectual. The harvest of it is always an earned harvest, and it is earned by an effort which is a discipline, a discipline not only of mind but also of character.

Nevertheless, after all has been said that can rightly be said in praise of Education, there remains the fact that some of the chief administrative qualities are not results of Education—at least, not of the Education that can be directly tested by an examination such as the Class I. Examination. No such Education can give tact; no such Education can make a feeble man capable of assuming or bearing responsibility. Natural capacity for administration is found in many grades of English life, and wherever found it has been developed by an experience which is wider than that of the class-room—by an experience of which one aspect has been designated "experience of life," and another, "social experience." The older English Universities afford opportunities for a valuable kind of social experience, and I have no doubt that much of the success of the Class I. Examination is a consequence of the fact that hitherto most of the candidates have had those or similar opportunities. Devised as an educational test, that examination has (to some extent) operated, not as a class-preference, but as a method of "group-selection" —as a method of selecting, and selecting from, a certain ethological group.

10. A school or university is a good recruiting-ground for the Administrative Civil Service, not merely because it educates up to a certain standard, but chiefly because it develops character and capacity through a certain kind of social experience. That experience, however, is made possible, not by the school or university itself, but by something brought into it. To find the primary conditions of the administrative capacity which it provides, one has to look far beyond its walls. In England much of the administrative capacity hitherto found in the older universities—which have furnished by far the larger number of candidates for the Class I. Examination—has been a result of nurture and training in a social *milieu* informed by a certain highly complex tradition. Young men so nurtured and trained have brought to their university the tradition which has made them what they are, and in the social experience afforded by the usages of the place that tradition has continued its characteristic work, forming and informing men apt to receive it although born outside it. The process has been one of ethological assimilation. It has not been confined within any one class; it has not been limited by the blurred lines of demarcation between different social classes.

Certain other things should also be borne in mind:

(1) The power of a small ethological group in a school or university to assimilate new elements is not unlimited. Indeed, it may easily be overtaxed.

(2) Well-known social and moral changes in English

> life have affected the formative power of the older universities. Moreover, the younger universities, with their new and almost untested forms of social experience, are daily becoming more and more important. Of those who now receive university training very many are strangers to the administrative tradition and not a few are ill-prepared to receive it.

These facts make it probable that the educational test which has succeeded hitherto, by concomitance, in selecting from the universities adequate recruits for the Administrative Civil Service will become less trustworthy. Consequently that test should be supplemented. I regret that the Commission has not been able to do more towards providing a supplement.

11. I am not satisfied with the last sentence in Section 42 of Chapter III.

Education by itself is not a sufficient preparation for administrative work. The fact that a boy is "clever" affords no sufficient ground for presuming that he will be a good administrator. Problems of administration are not wholly intellectual problems, and, in so far as they are of that kind, they do not hold the highest place. They make larger demands on character and manhood than they do on the intellect.

I believe that in order to reconcile "the interests of democracy with the interest of the public service" there must be given to "the democracy" not only better education, but also the opportunities of freedom and its duties in a more human, a more hopeful, a more invigorating social order.

APPENDIX IV

An Englishman's Thought of the Empire

Read at a meeting of Ceylonese held in London on the Sinhalese "National Day," 1918.

There is a widespread belief that the war-aims of the Allies involve or require a repudiation of imperialism. What, then, of the British Empire?

That august polity—built up and knit together by England's best life—has impassioned many with a great love. For them it has become the centre of a loyalty which goes down to the very foundations of faith and thought. "The idea of the Empire" is a chief information of their lives. What have they to do? Have they to tear that loyalty out of their hearts?—to burn what they adored? I am sure that they have not to do anything of the kind.

The imperialism which men are disavowing—in various approximations to insincerity—seems to be a form of *Macht-Politik*. It is a forcible imposition of sovereignty for selfish ends and uses. What have we to do with *that*—we Englishmen who are not afraid and not ashamed to avow that our patriotism is imperial? Nothing in the world.

For what is the British Empire? A far-extended power? Yes, but also something infinitely more. It is chiefly and distinctively *a supra-national organisation of freedom*—a unity which essentially intends "the Common Right established by our common human nature." Every particular assumed into that unity is taken up into an ethical system and a great experiment,—into a system constituted by the general *right to opportunity*, into an experiment towards the *freedom that is justice*. There you have the *meaning* of the Empire.

Deeds done under Eastern skies have stained the Empire's shield, vulgar hands have degraded the Empire's power, small minds have narrowed and deflected its policy, but there it stands—a peerless achievement, Asia's light, the safeguard of the world's best hope, of all earthly politics the one most worth living for and most worth dying for.

No misuse of it can annul the meaning of it.

APPENDIX V

THE MEANING OF THE EMPIRE

Reprinted from *The National Weekly.*

EARLY one summer's morning German armies violated the treaty-defended soil of Belgium, and England—mindful of her plighted word—sprang to arms. And England was not alone, for the unexpected trumpet-calls that rang out in England were carried by the winds of heaven to the four quarters of the world, and the *Empire* sprang to arms. We were told that we went to war for the sanctity of international law and the rightful liberties of small nations. These things are great, but something greater than these things moved us in those August days, when we uplifted ourselves above the pleasantness and profits of Peace to the high self-sacrifice of War. *The Motherland called us*, and, over thousands of miles of sea, distant sons of that august Mother—sons who had never seen her face—heard her voice and responded nobly. They came in their thousands from Canada, Australia, New Zealand—from every spot where the British Flag marks a home of Freedom and a sanctuary of Right. Why did they come? What impulse brought them, from their work and from their homes, to the fatal hills of Anzac and the shell-riven fields of France?

Something happened to them. What was it? Precisely what happened to Englishmen in the Homeland.

Before the war—we all know what England was like before the war. We were largely trivial, largely selfish, largely insincere. Neither politics, nor religion, nor work reached down to the depths of life. Not one of them moved the primary loyalties of human nature or engaged its fundamental veracity. Yet "the lordliest life on earth" had fashioned us, the greatness of England had nurtured us. But we knew it not, for our eyes were holden. Then came the war. The breath of God passed over these English lands, and the dormant life which held the greatness of a thousand years awoke. That month of August was a month of resurrection. And not only in England was it that. The greatness of England had not stayed at home. It had gone abroad, an unrecorded export, in the hearts of England's migrant sons, and in far-off Dominions it had worked as it worked at home—silently, in the foundations of character. Our English centuries were wrought into our distant kinsmen's lives. No one noticed that work, but when war broke out it was revealed. "One King, one Flag, one Empire!" Yes, and something else, without which those other things were little worth—*one life.* The war showed us that the Empire's primary unity subsists in a *common manhood.*

Here, in these English lands, we have made for ourselves a stately home, but the life which that home nurtures and enshrines is greater than the walls magnifical which protect it. Unresting through the long centuries, Freedom has been at work in the hearts and minds of Englishmen, and has built up for us a peerless tradition of free and serviceable manhood, of free manhood in a free State. Passing beyond the seas, in the train of various undertakings, it established itself in many lands, and to-day it knits together widely-sundered peoples by common memories and a common hope. Because of this, our Empire is more than a far-flung sovereignty, though this it is—more than a successful business, though this it must be. It is the embattled home of an ethical idea, of History's greatest achievement, of the Future's noblest possibility. By this imperial adventure our tradition has been enlarged, and now it lives in every quarter of the world as the thought and formative principle not merely of free manhood in a free State, but of free manhood in a free union of free States.

Freedom!—to us Englishmen that word is dear, for it designates our birthright and our life. Freedom is our country's characteristic greatness, the meaning of her history, her strength in the present,—an unused strength,—her hope for the future. Remote at first and obscurely seen, in the fullness of the days she visited the homes of men, and made for herself here and there a dwelling-place and a shrine. And, as time went on, her shelters and her altars multiplied. She went to and fro among the works of men; thousands who had worshipped her from afar beheld her unveiled face, and wherever she passed there sprang up a transforming hope and a deathless purpose. In her presence old enmities died down and the thoughts of men grew larger; her common benediction throbbed in their hearts as the first pulse of a new brotherliness. Men found in her the strength of life and its daily refreshment. Her increasing light became the dawn or the promise of a better day. And now? A people that has not known her has challenged her Right and assailed her work. To defend these things—to safeguard all that Freedom has wrought in and for the lives of nations—this free Empire of free men to-day bears unwonted arms. The unity of the Empire is evident to-day as a unity for Freedom.

For Freedom—is that the last word? No, it is not. We did not bring alien arms to Freedom's cause. Freedom has made us what we are—what we are at our best. We had given ourselves to unworthy things—to pleasure, to money-making, to the insincerities of party strife,—but deep in our hearts there was a manhood which these things did not engage. That fundamental manhood was the work of Freedom, and it was *this* manhood—the vital bond and common inheritance of the British peoples—that answered Freedom's call. The primary unity of the Empire is a unity *in* Freedom.

What do we mean by Freedom ? Freedom is opportunity to grow—not to grow selfishly, but to grow helpfully; to achieve (in character and purpose) the magnanimity of Patriotism and the broad equities of a general Right. *That* is what the British Empire stands for : *that* is the meaning of the Empire. The British Empire is the chief political assertion of the right to opportunity.

HAKLUYT EGERTON